# MY CONS(

Charlie,

You are a very positive person and a great colleague to work with.

Thank you for your time & efforts to make the teams in India more informed & integrated with the Institutional business.

Hope to see you again soon!

Aulolflal

4th Feb '16

# MY CONSCIENCE

*Auto writing by*
**Roshni and Sankalp Lal**

**Manjul Publishing House**

First published in India by

**Manjul Publishing House Pvt. Ltd.**
*Corporate Office*
2nd Floor, Usha Preet Complex,
42 Malviya Nagar, Bhopal 462 003 - India
Email: manjul@manjulindia.com
Website: www.manjulindia.com

*Sales and Marketing Office*
7/32, Ground Floor, Ansari Road, Daryaganj,
New Delhi 110 002 - India
Email: sales@manjulindia.com

*My Conscience* by *Roshni* and *Sankalp Lal*

Copyright © Roshni and Sankalp Lal 2014

This edition first published in 2014

**ISBN    978-81-8322-383-6**

Printed & bound in India by Thomson Press (India) Ltd.

*This book is dedicated to our loving parents
who gave us the abundant capacity to absorb
all that is new with an open mind.*

*We love you and thank you for loving us
the way you do...
Usha and Sansar Mohan Lal,
Sujata and Dilip Malaiya*

# Contents

# ROSHNI'S INTRODUCTION TO THE BOOK

Let me start by removing any confusion that you may have by the words 'Automatic Writing' or 'Auto Writing.' Auto writing is a process through which angels and guides communicate with humans to pass higher wisdom by telepathically making us read their thoughts and pen them down simultaneously. This connection, of our mind with their thoughts, directs us to inscribe their messages. Sankalp and I have been channelling their messages since mid-2010. This entire book has been auto written. Let me also tell you that this is not the first book that has been auto written. There are a lot of great books that are already in circulation since many years. In fact, had you mentioned the word auto writing to us about a couple of years ago – we, too, would have asked what it was all about and then probably searched the Internet to find out more. The concept maybe new to a lot of people but the practice is far from 'new.'

We were not initiated or taught or told by anyone that we had to auto write. And that's the beauty of it. It just *happened* to us.

We first came to know about it when a relative of ours started auto writing. We went to her with curiosity and awe and asked if she would write something for us. We were astonished at how fast her hand moved and at the words that were being written. The messages were so pure and true that we felt as though she inculcated the spirit of God Himself. While she wrote for another relative of ours, we were shocked at the accuracy of the answers. That relative happened to ask from the angels about how his work was going and whether he was in the right job or not. And bang came the reply – "What work? You don't have a job."

We were shocked because later on he told us that he had not been going to work since the past few months though he had not told anyone about it.

This made us realise that the angels knew everything and also confirmed that they would have an answer to everything.

After a few months, Sankalp suddenly started having an urge that I auto write. There was this 'calling' which came from somewhere deep within him. Initially, this urge was faint but slowly, it started welling up. He started to insist that I do it. Naturally, I found the whole idea preposterous and refused point blank. It was difficult for me to concur, as according to me, this was something that only saints or highly spiritual people with some kind of mystical powers could achieve. It was not something *I* could do! Why would *they* want to connect with *me*? I did not have any knowledge or skill or even the inclination, to tell you the truth. I was happy being awestruck by someone else's achievement and that was the extent to which I wished to stay!

He, however, kept insisting and to get him off my back I suggested that he wrote first. How was I to know that he would be able to! And that too so effortlessly!

Let me take a moment to explain to you how it is done, before moving on to my experience.

What you are supposed to do is hold a pen lightly on top of the paper, without touching the paper. So it looks as though you are ready to start writing. You begin by concentrating on what you have to do and meditating. You offer a little prayer that you be connected to the higher guides and masters and that you are well protected at all times with their love and light. Our relative had told us earlier about all of this so we kind of knew what to do. Once we concentrated, we could feel a different kind of energy rushing through us and felt our minds go blank. While auto writing our thoughts are put on hold so we are able to channel what the guides have to say to us. So, in other words, we could start reading their minds. Most of the times we don't remember what we have written as we only concentrate on writing and do not analyse or use logic in deciphering the message as it would break our connection with the guides and we would begin to write what 'we' think instead of following the dictation that they give us. It is imperative that we let our mind and logic take a hike while we connect to the higher spirits in order to get accurate messages. We had been meditating and doing various workshops on Past Life Regression with Dr Newton Kondaveti and that was what prepared us to open ourselves up and be able to connect directly with our guides and masters in the spirit world.

Since the beginning, Sankalp would connect easily and effortlessly to these guides and masters. He connected instantly and fluently wrote what was being channelled through him. He has always been a slow writer so I was amazed at the speed with which he wrote when connected. This encouraged me to write but it was a rather scary start for me. When I began to concentrate initially, my hand held on to the pen as if my life depended on it. I just could not let go of it. Whenever I sat to practice writing I would start drawing circles on a page or at times continuously wrote gibberish, which did not even come close to being identified with any alphabet that I knew about. Most of the times there was just scribbling and sometimes, due to the immense energies I felt, the pages would even tear because of the force with which my pen moved. At the end of the beginning, I had basically finished off a couple of registers without making a single proper sentence.

In one instance, the pen fell from my hand and my hand reacted as a fish would without water. During this time I was certain that something evil had possessed me. We quickly sent an email to Dr Newton (he is the one we turn to for any spiritual guidance) to query about what was happening. To our surprise and relief, he assured us that it was normal and that we were on the right track.

So, that is how our journey with the masters began. Even after hundreds of incidents, the experience still amazes us. We have since written with a lot of different angels and guides. At times we even connected with our relatives and friends who had passed on. The way we write with each angel is different; our handwriting changes and our comfort level is also more with some when we write with them regularly. There is a difference in the vibrations we receive when connected with some higher souls or masters. In a few instances we even connected directly with the source/God and the energies we felt during those times were immense. The book also holds a chapter that has been narrated by God.

No matter who makes us write, the one common thing is that their words are of pure love and always so encouraging. I say this because we have not been very consistent in putting efforts to write regularly and have not kept our promises with them many times. Yet they are forgiving and unconditional in their love. They do show their annoyance and give us a piece of their mind when we neglect our duties but at the same time they also encourage us to go ahead and keep writing. Their sternness at such times only motivates us to come back to our senses and connect with them at a deeper level.

Initially, we both wrote answers only for each other's questions. We were not too sure how others would react to what we had started doing, so we kept this knowledge to ourselves. Gradually, our family members started asking questions through us and when they realised how accurate the answers were, we got motivated and encouraged to continue writing.

All in all, our experience while writing with them has always given us direction as well as the confidence of where to go and what to do.

## LET US TELL YOU HOW THEY ARE!

They are our best friends. We could discuss any and everything with them. They always give us sound advice. They always listen to us and boost our confidence when we need it the most.

Humorous, they would crack jokes or one-liners, just as we do with one another. Once, Sankalp had had a couple of beers so wasn't sure if he could still auto write. When he sat down to write, our dear friend William said/wrote, 'You can write! You may be drunk but I'm not!'

They are an ocean of patience...in fact, all oceans combined! My brother usually has just one question to ask from them. Every time he asked it, I got exasperated by the repeated question. Yet, the angels replied to the same question with such seriousness and attention each time that I was astounded by their tolerance level.

They are witty and charming, they are wise and smart. The angels and guides know us all inside out so you cannot hide anything from them. They know your questions and they know the answers.

Meticulous in their instructions, they will tell you in detail what you should or should not do. At other times they may have the simplest of solutions to your most complicated questions.

Gentle in their approach, they know how to deal with each one of us in a manner we would find most receptive. At the same time, they are always encouraging and persuasive. If there is something they want you to know or do, they will repeatedly give you messages, in various forms, to do it.

One thing they are not, at anytime or in any circumstance is – angry. They can be strict, firm or very direct in their communication but they will never get upset or unhappy or angry about anything you may do. How ever stern they may seem, they would not let you be without telling you exactly what you are doing wrong and would also show you how to correct yourself. At times, they push you to your limit but not without showing you all the hurdles with the ways to cross them.

There are so many of these beautiful beings, everywhere and for everyone, at all times!

## WOULD YOU LIKE TO KNOW HOW THEY MIGHT APPEAR?

Fine suspended glitter – that is what they look like and each angel has a different colour/shade. Some are pink, some purple or golden, silver, white...and they don't have any particular form. They can't!

Can you imagine some gas trapped in a gas cylinder? Do you think the gas would take the form of a cylinder? No; it would still be gas...moving around without a form. And if the gas were to be let out, then what form would it have? It would just spread, wouldn't it? It would be everywhere but still be gas. That is how it is with them. They are particles of energy – spread everywhere.

Here is a brief description about all the guides that have written this book.

## ARCHANGEL MICHAEL

He is all around and is here to protect all of mankind on this earth plane. You will always experience and feel his presence when you face challenging situations. He will be around those who need help. He can transform the way clouds take shape and can make mountains collapse. He is with those who feel weak and also with those who help the weak. His method of interaction is simple – just take his name and he will interact with you.

## GOD

God is the pure energy that has not yet disintegrated and the energy that accepts the particles back to it. God is the source as well as the destination of each and every soul.

## WILLIAM

He is an evolved soul and a permanent member of our (Sankalp's and my) soul group. He has shared many lifetimes with us and is dedicatedly helping us to fulfil our destiny.

He has taken many births on the earth plane and his last birth was of a significant yogi who wrote an autobiography. We can always feel his presence around the two of us.

## TOM

He is best known as a free spirit in between two earth lives. His message comes from his understanding of the wrong doings of his last life.

## FRANCINE E. KRISHNA

She was my Nani (maternal grandmother) who had passed on when I was in college. I was really close to her and every time she comes to write with us I can feel her love and energies surrounding us. Once when Sankalp was writing with nani, I was just thinking to myself how much I missed her hugs. I had not said it out loud but Sankalp automatically wrote that nani too missed hugging me! It was a beautiful moment for me.

## SOLORIS

Soloris or the God of Sun has written a lot of messages contained in this book. I am extremely comfortable writing with him and feel at peace every time he comes.

We hope we have done justice to what they wanted to be conveyed and that you will take full advantage of the words that have been written for you.

# SANKALP'S JOURNEY

Have you ever had that feeling that you didn't belong anywhere or didn't fit-in with the rest? Or had that nagging urge to do something different but not know exactly what? Well, this was my story for as long as I can remember...

I belong to a highly educated and cultured family. My elder brother had chosen his line of career and was an engineer. I however never knew what I wanted to do. Though I have always come across as an individual with a strong personality I started having doubts in my abilities – feeling as though I didn't belong where I was.

Due to the age gap between my parents and me, we could not understand each other to that level which was required at that time. I needed someone to guide me and show me the right path but felt as though I did not have anyone to turn to. While in school, the feeling of not belonging grew as the years progressed.

After passing out from school I did not know what I would be good at or what would interest me. I had scored very well and could have got admission to any college of my choice. I however, chose the field of hotel management just to get away from the subjects I had studied in school. But the feeling of not belonging and not heading in the right direction peaked during the three year course.

I was miserable and felt I needed a guide, a saviour to tell me what I needed to do for everything to fall in place. After a short stint with hotels I finally took a firm stand to change my field of work and got into Business Process Outsourcing, which was an up and coming avenue at the time but was frowned upon as a concrete career option.

Even though I received instant success and respect in this field, I was unable to enjoy my success due to lack of self-worth. My desire for a guide kept growing.

A few years later, after a tragedy in my family, I became curious about incarnation and life after death, which led me to Dr Newton, a great master in the art of **Past Life Sciences**. Through him I learned various concepts of life patterns, karmic cycles as well as how to be aligned to *my* purpose of life. During one of Dr Newton's workshops, I experienced and re-lived my own birth.

I realized that I had been carrying the need for me to have a guide or another source of help since the time of my birth. I experienced my birthing process, which was via a C-section where artificial help was being extended to help me make my way out from my mother's womb. While re-living this experience, I understood something very profound and realized that it was not *I* that had needed the external help but it was my mother's body that had needed help as it was incapable to deliver me in the natural way.

*This message completely changed my life.*

I started understanding the patterns that occurred in other areas of my life like, why my father fell ill when I needed him, why I had chosen a career path which was uncommon at the time and felt nobody could help me. I realised that neither my parents nor the world around me could build me up. I had to be the driver of my own life. Auto writing happened to me right after the rebirth experience. The messages I received through auto writing told me to believe in *me*. I am now a completely changed person from within, yet the same person to the outside world. I have now started believing in myself and thus can confidently tell you that you can believe me and what has been written in this book (through me).

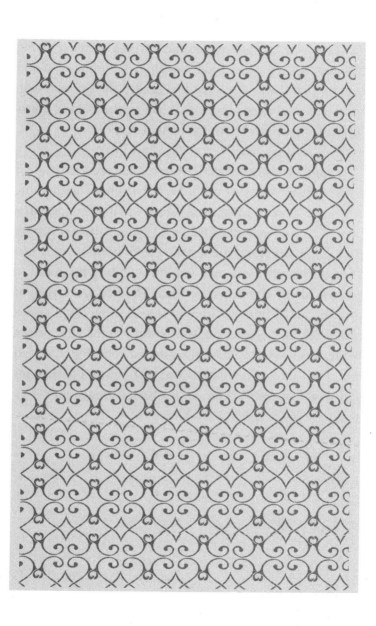

# INTRODUCTION
## *by the Angels*

Have you wondered – why we have taken birth on this earth plane? There are many answers. The Bible says 'to follow God's will', The Quran says 'to be with God' and The Gita says 'to be around your friends and fellow mankind'. All of them are close, yet none hits the nail on the head.

We (souls) take shape into a body on the earth plane to experience what GOD wants us to experience – good and bad, easy and difficult, beautiful and ugly. Why do you think we need such experiences? Because we can't understand 'good' unless we know 'bad', we can't understand light unless we see and experience darkness. All kinds of experiences are required for us to be able to reach the stage where we are today.

However, it is with much trepidation that I have to tell you that all you have lived for up-till now is just the beginning. This game that you have started is so fun-filled and adventurous that you would never want it to end. So it goes on for better or worse but always as per how *you* choose it to be.

✱

This book is about the many kinds of people that we have seen in our lives. If not directly, we would have seen all the events mentioned in this book happen to someone or the other. The events or situations that directly relate to us will be the ones that need to be marked or underlined because these are the chapters you will need to read again and again after periods of time so that you (*i*) don't forget how you ended up in the situation that you are in and, (*ii*) learn how you can get out of it. You can keep unmarking the pages as and when a particular situation completely vanishes. You will feel a sense of achievement in doing so.

You must have surely been told time and again that 'life is no joke' – yet, you never listened to it and treated life as a joke. The message has been sent to you time and again. This book is yet another one. Life really is no joke. You can laugh at yourself, but not at what you have done to yourself.

The conclusion that you wish to draw from the above question will make you realise if this book is indeed for you or for those who do not take life seriously. But what difference would that make? You still have to read on because it is 'your' conscience that we are going to talk about and I know for sure that *it* will not let you keep this book down, even if you try very hard. It will resurface every now and then till you read it. Just like the many messages you get but do not think about unless they stare right in the face.

So, we will then come a full circle. You would be in the same category you thought you wouldn't be in (not taking the messages you get seriously – not taking *life* seriously)!

You will be blessed by the words in this book and with the thorough understanding of what the world at large is all about. It will be a great experience to have you read this book and make you realise what you have been doing wrong.

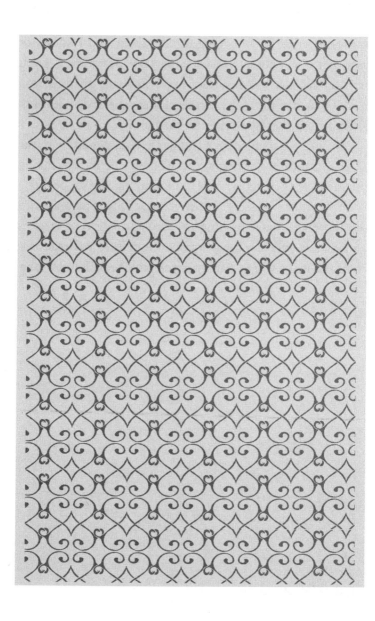

We urge our readers to please read the introductions before beginning with the chapters as this would give you a clear understanding of the 'Unseen Force' that made us write this book.

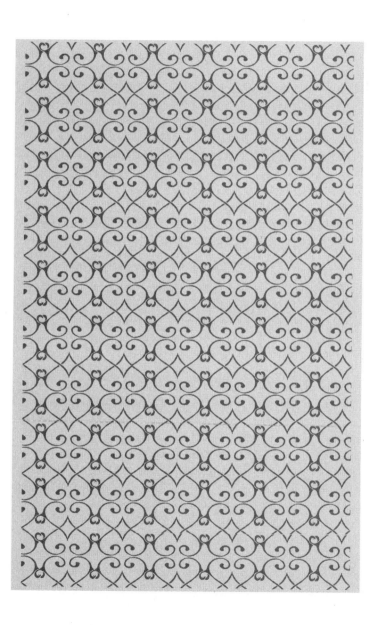

# 1

# Your Conscience:
# Where It All Started!

*The message below has been given by William*

The world at any one point of time has never been the same. Many changes have taken place to make us understand what we know as the truth. It all began when the source of light and energy started to feel ignorant of the light and energy it possessed. This led to God forming different particles from the source to come out and live independently. The power each particle possessed, as a particle, was so powerful and luminous that it made God experience what powers he really possessed.

The Gods have two kinds of powers. They can either be or they can just 'let it be'. Since they choose to do the first they have decided to do the latter with their forms. This is what free will is all about.

I will elaborate.

## THE 'TO BE' STATE

This state existed when there was just the stillness of the entire cosmos all around and when there was nothing but the one and only thing called energy. There were no feelings, no love, no hatred – no nothing. This energy source just existed; without any movement, without any thought, without any purpose. It was bored...so bored that it decided to entertain itself by forming an elaborate game-plan so that it never got bored again. The game-plan, it thought, had to be foolproof and had to be super perfect so that it always required its attention and involvement. Up till now, the energy was in the 'to be' state.

The game-plan was to disintegrate itself into many particles to spread itself throughout the entire cosmos. It wanted each particle to have a full and complete 'life', i.e. to know, to live, to understand and to experience. All these were spread widely and they started their journey from where they were at that point of time. The particles had now begun their own evolution. As they grew and understood more and more about themselves, they went on to become particles of the various minerals that we find in today's world.

Every mineral lives for many a thousand years before it degenerates. In that period of time, it sees and senses a lot of things. It needs to understand the knowledge before it starts to experience it. This is the slowest and most gradual way in which it starts coming into being. It still has many stages to go through, and to go through those, this stage is most appropriate and necessary for it to be better prepared for what is to come. This stage shows reliability on the self and more than anything, the strength of longevity. Self-being and self-confidence of its existence start from here.

Now, in order for it to experience 'what it feels', the mineral then becomes a plant or a seed. Here the journey of just being stable or motionless ends. A new journey, a new chapter, begins, and a new dress (in the form of a plant) is worn by the particle, so to say. This same particle that came from the 'source', after having lived many years as plant/s or tree/s and collecting the many profound experiences of growth, vitality and change, then transforms itself to the animal form. Animals of all shapes and sizes. They learn what mobility is and also how to rest, i.e. to go into an immobile state for lengths of time. The true balance of mobility is learnt while in the animal form, from being a cheetah to a turtle or a snail, from birds to fish, from a snake to an octopus, etc.

Every form has its learning. But the journey couldn't have been complete if this was all there was. We needed to understand that survival was not the only reason for existence of the self or the species. When a soul transitions from the animal level to human form, it has massive animal powers that remain dormant. The lesson of interaction and action starts hereafter. The more people it (the particle) met the more circumstances it created and the more emotions it felt and thus the more experiences it gained. Many, many lifetimes were required for it to come to a stage where it could see things from a different point of view – the point of view of a person who watches from high above and understands the nature of things and how they work. The 'human form' then grew and grew from one planet to another, from one galaxy to another, from one universe to another. It took many lives, many shapes, to experience how to live fully.

Each particle will live the complete cycle, not even a single particle will be left behind as, ultimately, all particles need to start the process of integrating back into the source. So, every experience – new or old, every thought – good or bad, will make us reach there faster. That is our personal goal – goal of the particle from the source. Once we are together (integrated back to the source) again, we will decide once more what game is to be played next.

But remember, this is not a game where one comes first or even last. It is a game of our own journey – how fast we learn and how fast we grow. All will reach there sooner or later and if you happen to be there first, then you will have to wait for the others to join you. Therefore, make everyone aware of what you learn about yourself (through this book and otherwise) so that others can also be helped and can hasten their growth and journey towards the source. This way, once you are there you will not have to wait too long for the others to join you.

## THE 'LET IT BE' STATE OR FREE WILL

Once the particle is disjointed from the source, the source does not hinder or interfere with its progress. For example, once in the human form, the source will not tell us what to do or what not to do. It will not show us what we need to do in order to learn our lessons and gain our experiences. It will not punish us for being 'bad'. It will just let us be, the way we want ourselves to be.

Our conduct will be our own at all times and will not be 'God's will'. This is known as free will. I will explain it with yet another example: A man is waiting to cross the road when the traffic signal is red. Once it turns green, it is his option to cross the road or to keep standing where he is for as long as he wants to. It is his will (his *free will*) to do what he wants to do. If there were no free will, God would not have experienced so many experiences (through each one of us). If he wanted to dictate our lives, what would be his experience?

Most experiences come from adventures and not from rules or discipline. So God has 'let us be' how ever we want to be so we can grow at a pace that we feel comfortable with. Each one's pace is different and each one's progress is different. We are all the same particles that are spread across everywhere. We come from the same source with the same purpose and with the same intent. Some have already joined back to the source, some are on the journey back to the source and some have no clue about it at all. But all will get there, one by one. As a person gets back home after a long, exciting yet exhausting adventure, we will all meet as one in that source we all call home!

## KNOW WHERE YOU COME FROM

Few things are left unsaid about the human/soul evolution. Like, what was there before anyone (human) took birth? Animals? Correct! What was there before animals? Plants? Correct. Minerals? Correct. And what was there before minerals? Answer to the last query is energy. There was an abundance of energy with different capabilities that then took the shape of different minerals. The wide variety of minerals is due to the variety of energy found in the source. From minerals, evolution took them to become plants.

Different plants come into being from different minerals. The sheer variety and longevity of each plant differentiates it on the basis of what it has come from. Plants are static creatures that learn to endure and see the world. They give life to other creatures (oxygen) and will seldom ever cause any disturbance. The falling of a tree could be an example, when their endurance goes beyond a point.

Plants evolved into single cellular animals. The single cell grew into two and thus evolution took us to the current state of the rise of human kind. The human kind is very advanced; it has learnt many lessons of the past centuries by being minerals, plants and animals. Humans know at a subconscious level what is it like to be all those things and how it is to live a life with all the learnings from their previous incarnations in different forms.

Is there a more advanced race than humans? Sure, there is. It's called the 'conscious human'. A creature who knows the game of life and the rules to play it. I am sure I have disappointed you with the above answer if you were looking for mutants/aliens. It is not necessary to talk about anything apart from humans for the purpose of this book. I may bring this topic up at another time/book.

What's the difference between a 'conscious human' and any other type? The difference is that for conscious humans, what counts is not the importance they get in their current lives, but the importance they give to the purpose of their lives. Both these types go about living their life, learning and growing as they go along; so what difference does it make if a person is conscious or not? Most of you will agree with me when I say that it does matter. However, at the back of your mind, you may have a question that when we do a task very well without knowing the rules, then why make things complicated by spelling out every permutation and combination of doing things in the task? The person who knows all aspects of the situation is the one who would be most vulnerable about his decision to choose one way amongst many. The person who understands the most appropriate approach and walks the path of that approach is able to fully succeed in accomplishing that task that is necessary for the soul's journey and evolution.

## SOUL PURPOSE

*Message given by Archangel Michael*

There are a few people who walk on this planet to spread their knowledge of the unknown. The unknown is the simplest thing to understand and follow. The unknown for most of us is – how do we end up in the same situations again and again? How do we pass over? Where do we go? Will my present actions have an effect on my future? Will I always be like this? Will there be a path that will take me out of this routine? Does God decide our destiny or does karma have an effect? How does karma start and why?

The unknowns are plenty in our heads and most of these questions can be understood by just one statement. That is, we have decided what we want to experience in this life. We are in need to live what is necessary for us to complete the journey of our existence. Our destiny is to complete the full journey and we will always get reminders about how to complete the learning's of this life. So what we see as obstacles are the 'reminders'. The reason we run away from our obstacles is that we want to run away from our path, the will and the purpose of our life. We need to ask ourselves, what learning do 'I' gain from the experience that I am getting.

By fulfilling your purpose of this life you don't immediately pass over. Instead, you make more progress on other experiences that are out there to be undergone. The very straight path to God has become complicated and absurd because of the many versions and customs associated with it. Once we pass over, we are taken back to the source where it all started. We journey back to see glimpses of all lost opportunities and the hurdles we overcame. There is a stock of everything we needed to do and we mark each point as done or to be redone. The ones to be 'redone' get added to the list for the next life. The extra lessons learnt get subtracted from it as well.

So, my dear friend, we have the power to observe what is bothering us and we have the universe to let us know what lessons we need to learn each day. We are going to be able to accomplish many lives worth of experiences in this life if we are open and allow new things into our lives. If there is anything that obstructs us we know there is a learning to be had. Most times people choose to do what other people expect them to do. The core thought of being somewhere or doing something is what makes a person happy or unhappy. So, whatever situation that you are in right now, if you are not happy then it is because what you have done is according to the needs and wants and wishes of others who really 'matter' to you. But really think about it. Do they matter or do you matter more? If your answer is you, than re-evaluate and redo a lot of things to straighten your life and start being a happy person. Others won't give it to you; you need to manufacture your own happiness.

*Message given by William*

The flower that blooms with the world is the flower that we hold in our hands everyday. It is the flower of wisdom and knowledge. As much as we learn there is still more to learn. Why is that? Have you ever wondered? Why is there so much more to know, to learn, to absorb, to love, to endure? We feel that the course is really very vast and that it is simply impossible for one to learn about everything that there is in one life. So to solve this, there are many lifetimes given to each of us. To learn and also to unlearn. Furthermore with each life we take, we feel that there is more to explore, to unearth, to discover, to imagine. So we go on and on, with this adventure of exploration.

Many lives we take to build our beliefs and then, in some, we ourselves break those beliefs. It is all a game we like to play, sometimes seriously and most times for fun. This, however, we only realise once we have passed on after each life that we live on the earth.

Now imagine, if we feel that the course is so vast then how vast must it feel for God himself? There are so many galaxies and so much more that the source is overwhelmed with all kinds of possibilities and wants us to explore and delve deeper and deeper into our wants and desires so it (the source) can benefit from our understanding. The more we experience, the more full the source feels because it is us that make up the source. We are parts of the source, each one of us. Each part is equally important to the source because of the immense knowledge and experience we bring to the source. All needs to be experienced, the best and the worst of all aspects, and only then will we be complete, only then would we have understood who we really are and where we really come from.

You will have realised by now that the souls' purpose is to reunite the knowledge and the experiences in such a manner that neither is different from the other. The understanding is so complete that at human levels we feel the soul stirred by this knowledge and at the soul level the experience makes it (the soul) much fuller, whole and complete.

In the event of a death, a person generally would seek the help of the Akashik* records of the one who has passed

---

*Akashik records are described as containing all knowledge of human experience and the history of the cosmos. They are metaphorically described as a library; other analogies commonly found in discourse on the subject include a "universal supercomputer" and the "Mind of God". People who describe the records assert that they are constantly updated automatically and that they can be accessed through astral projection or when someone is placed under deep hypnosis.

on. But in the event of a lifetime, the records do not make much sense, as what will happen can always be changed and re-scripted due to the beautiful power of free will.

You may question here – why don't we get along with our fellow souls when everybody has taken shape from the same source? Why is there anger in the world? Why don't we live in peace? Why can't all religions coexist in harmony? Why, why? Well, to understand this, you first need to think about your own progress from a child to an adult.

The bitterness you had with your teachers when they tried to teach you something new and difficult. Reflect back to the same teacher now and you have so much admiration for the same person. This is our understanding level of what is necessary for our growth in terms of knowledge and experience. For a soul, a lifetime is like a level/class in school. There are various subjects to learn and practice and the pass marks are 100 per cent. Even if you leave an aspect of the subject now, you would need to redo the subject entirely (like a retest!).

When starting out as a human, the soul is young and fresh. So, we may call it a baby soul which then goes on to become a young soul, an adult soul and a mature (conscious) soul. And after that it is an enlightened soul. To further explain: when a soul is in the animal form it sees, feels, hears, endures and survives a lot. Only after it has gained enough experiences and emotions after being born as different types of animals/creatures does it transform into a human soul. And that is how, once we are full of such experiences and knowledge, that we move on to the next level of the soul group.

So my dears, why is there so much hatred? The more we grow in number the more baby souls emerge. Their understanding is that they can survive only when they are a part of a clan and fight all others outside the clan. For them, the correct way of survival is the lesson they need to learn. For these souls to understand that the world is a safe place, they need to undergo many lifetimes of experience to reach the stage of a young soul. Once they reach this stage, they know that the world is safe. However, they don't understand the balance necessary. So they end up being too self-centred and flamboyant or too introverted. The politicians, the actors, the media persons who try and impose their ideas on peoples' minds are of these kinds. The spiritual gurus who are rigid in their thought process are in this community too. When the experiences of living the life of a superstar and a 'nobody' are complete, the souls reach a stage of an adult soul, meaning they have learnt the art of living a balanced life.

Now you may think this is an easy stage. Well, if you do, then you are very far from the truth. Once we know what is correct for us we can't ignore the fact that difficult ways need to be walked upon. Until we realise what we need to do, situations (and often disastrous situations) keep getting created to remind us of what we need to do. There are no in-betweens, all barriers need to be crossed and you cannot leave any stone unturned. You can't sit idle and watch your life go by. You need to take charge of each aspect and shape yourself in a manner that each and every pattern in your life is understood and dealt with. As they say – with great understanding comes greater responsibility.

What comes after we have achieved the ever so difficult 'balance'? Well, then comes the stage to show the path for others to reach the same stage. Spreading the message of 'rules' to live a joyful life. These people are either ridiculed or loved deeply but they leave a lasting impression on the lives of the people they touch. The celebrities who are humble and have an open mindset are amongst this group. While they may not spread the message in so many words as Buddha or Jesus, they are examples people like to follow. Buddha and Jesus are the same soul; they are the stage nearest to the source. They form the source yet they can detach from the source at free will and take shape again and again to come to earth and spread true knowledge. They uplift the souls of those who need guidance, they protect the ones who seek their help and fight the negativities so that the path to the source is cleared.

May I remind you, dear reader, that you are a learned being and as you read forward I would like you to stop and remember the things that you have read till now. My advice for the way of reading this book will be that you read it very slowly. Like a snail that crawls on a leaf and by the time it reaches the end of the leaf, it is aware of all the veins, colours and textures of the leaf. Be that snail. Devote just 10–15 minutes on the book everyday. Read just one or two paragraphs. But remember the book the entire day, throughout the night and even until the next day.

You are not in a marathon race to finish a book that you have started reading. That's not your goal. Your goal is to absorb all that is in the book. Once absorbed, it will be easy to live the way you feel as right. So read slowly and make life that much simpler and easier for yourself. It is for improvement purposes – this book. What you learn and how you learn from it is in your hands – it's your free will.

– *Soloris*

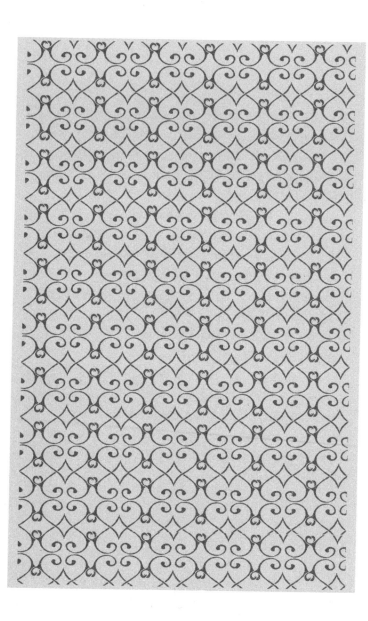

# 2

# The Game of Life

*Message given by William*

The life long agonies of what one faces are many. But has anyone ever thought why are these agonies to deal with in the first place? Imagine a place where there was only laughter and kindness and well being. No greed, no hate, no war, no crime. What would you call such a place – heaven? But guess what? The heaven that you call on earth – Kashmir (India), is full of things that you will not find in heaven! Ever wondered about this?

This is a prime example of what and where heaven really

is. Heaven is right here in your hearts, in your world. Where 'you' live, in what you do. Do it right and with love – you are always in heaven or will feel heavenly. Do it with hate and with greed – you are on earth, the same place where heaven is, but for you it'll always just be earth – where *you* think you have to always fight for survival.

There could be many reasons why things go against us. However, we choose to ignore them or fail to identify them. We tell ourselves that it is destiny, karma or plain luck; we have been trained to think that it's not in our control. I say everything is in our control. Each day and night is a figment of our innermost desire. There is nothing else to it. If where we need to go is clear in our mind and the obstacles from within are released, we could fly and reach our destination. We can't go wrong or fail.

Did you ever realise that all your failures were not because we didn't see them coming but because we knew that they may/could happen someday. If they didn't happen so far then something is amiss or I am too unworthy of it. For you 'taking things as they come' means accepting everything that life throws at you. Failure, sorrow, responsibility; but the real meaning to the same can be understood by the following story:

'There was once a boy of age 19. His parents were wealthy and he was their only son. They made their money by cutting grass and making hay for building houses. The boy was always well-behaved and loved. He respected his parents very much. The boy was about to turn 20 when his father told him "Son,

I am going to die very soon because of a deadly disease and you will need to take care of the business and your mother." The boy understood his responsibility and started going to their workplace and helped his father in the medical treatment that was necessary.

Then one day, his father told him "Son I want to see you married before I die. Please marry my friend's daughter who is of the same age as you are." The son felt a bit uptight as he had never met this girl before. However, to keep his father's wish, he accepted the girl's hand in marriage. Soon they were married and the father passed away after a couple of months.

The son took care of everything. He ensured that the factory was running properly and took care of the family. However, he felt he had made no choice of his own in his life so far and felt unhappy that he had had to accept things as they stood and that it was his destiny and duty as a son to lead his life in the circumstances created. Though the son did everything right, he was not happy.

On seeing this, his mother one day spoke to his wife. She asked what was going on with them, were they doing OK and if there was any problem. The wife said that her husband was a thorough gentleman and treated her well, but could not accept her as his wife. She said, "He has not accepted me as his own and he doesn't like what he does at work. He always feels bothered about the fact that he did not have a choice."

The mother was very wise; she went up to her son and asked him for some money. Without any questions, the son gave her the money. Next day, she asked for some more money and the son gave that too, smilingly. This continued for a couple of weeks, after which the son at last asked her why she needed so much money. The mother told him it was for her future.

The next few days also went by like this – the mother asked for the money and the son obliged. After almost a month, the son told his mother that he could not continue giving away money like this. He said that he was ready to support her in the future but couldn't keep on giving her money like this. The mother told him, "OK son, I have full faith in you to take care of me. I won't ask for any more money now." The son was surprised at this and asked her what she had done with all the money. She told him that she had put it all in her cupboard and now she would give it all back to him.

The son was further astonished, and questioned his mother as to why she hadn't asked a straight question earlier if she was insecure about him taking care of her in the future. The mother said, "I knew you would, son, but I wanted to see how you would react. Would you accept giving me money or take it in your hands to decide what you need to do with the money to ensure we have a secure future. You came out with flying colors. If only you had taken this stand when your father was alive you would have been so much happier." The son was puzzled and replied, "But mother, I had no choice." To this she replied, "You had a choice son, had you only asked what was needed from you under the situation. Your father had asked if you could take over his factory. The need from you was to have a way of earning to support yourself and me. Unwillingly, you accepted that running the factory was the only available choice. Similarly, when your father wanted to see you married and suggested a girl, you agreed. Who and how could have been in your hands but you didn't seek any choice in the matter. Son, what you did for your father and me is a spectacular example for other sons. However, not accepting your decisions will keep you unhappy and will keep all of us unhappy forever. The only way we can 'take things as they come' is by understanding what your role is and then doing what suits you best. You should stand up and demand things that you need to help you meet that role effectively with the backing of your heart.'

The story should make things clear about how to face challenging situations. If you still feel helpless in a situation, reread this story. The way the son chose to fulfill his fathers' will was in his own hands. His choice was difficult and did not seem right to his heart, even then he went along. If you ever land up in a similar situation, please always follow your heart and do things that make you feel good. There is a foolproof way of listening to your heart and it has been covered in a different chapter.

It is your own destiny that you have to fulfil. God has not decided upon your destiny but you have. You decided upon it because you knew that it was possible for you to achieve it. So nothing that you are experiencing – good or bad – is out of course. You had decided everything and now you are doing what you were meant to be doing.

Let's then take stock of the things that you really are doing and whether you are doing them well or not. Now at every workplace, there are performers who reach the expected mark and some who fall under it as well as a few who are above it. Without me telling you, you would understand what the 'above expectations' category of people may be doing and also by what is being missed by the 'under achievers'. This is how your life is – your performance – in your thoughts and actions – will determine where you currently stand. Your destiny could be very bad but are you capable enough to change it, to re-script what you had planned to do before you came to the earth plane? No, maybe not. Not many people will be able to do it. Yet here we really don't want destiny to change because this is the path that we have decided to embark upon in this lifetime. What we can do is learn our lessons wholeheartedly to not make the same mistakes again and again and again.

Once you are doing the right thing, you will understand your life's purpose. Whether it is good or bad, you have to make the most of it to be able to reach the 'exceeded expectations' mark. You would be duly rewarded once you complete this life. Only then will you know the growth you have made in all spheres because of the way you thought and behaved.

★

The wings sharpen their feathers and the feathers
soften themselves,
As each flight is taken, nowhere, somewhere, anywhere.
The birds do not know of this.
But this is what makes them fly.
Even in the coldest of days, even in the sunniest of skies.
The sharpness and the softness together as one – make
them fly.

The wings have the role to direct the flight of the bird in the
direction it wants to go. The role of the wing is to ensure that
the complete body of the bird is in a form to be able to do
what its brain and heart command: ascend, descend, turn, etc.
The feathers are instructed to take and hold the shape until
the turn is taken. Sharp feathers help the bird fly smoother
and faster. The feathers alone have a responsibility to keep
the birds warm and waterproof. Their purpose is different
when fulfilling their own destiny as against when they are
helping something else fulfil its destiny.

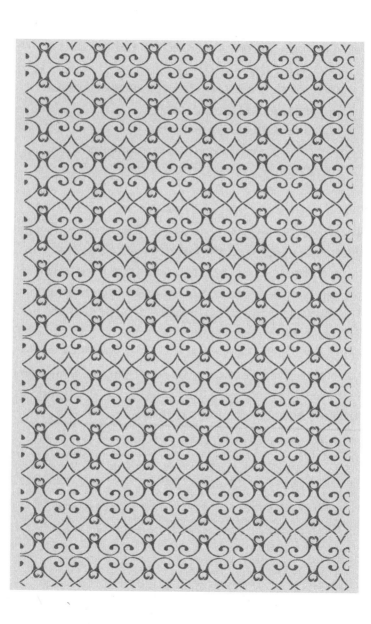

# 3

# Karma

*Message given by Francine E. Krishna*

After we die and before we take birth again, we write the next life journey to be taken. This would contain a list of super karmas that we have carried from the previous life and a set of new karmas.

The karmas are what we have decided to come with in this life by planning it all in the state previous to taking birth. Super karma is what we know we are going to carry from this life into the next because once we are aware of what karma is; we can choose to believe it or not believe it. But if you do believe in it, then there is no chance that you can ignore it. So if you do not understand the lessons in this life, you will have to learn them in much more elaborate terms in the next one. That is because you know about your mistake but you neglect to rectify it. So you are basically carrying a double karma that increases the load on yourself in your next life.

What you are doing here is God's work. Don't be under the impression that you are doing things only for yourself and for your personal upliftment. It is not just 'you' (as you know yourself) that needs help and enlightenment but all the others who form a part of you as well as God himself. You are on a mission here to pull up your socks and rectify your acts once you come to know about how the system works. But you are not allowed to ignore what you have learnt so far without dire implications on your next lives. So be careful of the words you choose to say and be careful of the thoughts you choose to think.

## HOW DO WE MAKE OUR OWN PATTERNS?

There are many occasions that come in each person's life that make him sit and think about what he has done to deserve what he is facing in his life. Emotions at such points are so strong yet at the same time, logic is extremely weak. He assures himself in his self-pity then starts to feel very small and insignificant but will not allow himself to see the problem or the crux of the matter in full detail. Such people are self-absorbed people who at such points in life can only think of how much smaller they can get emotionally and mentally. It is understandable that a person can be sad or disheartened over a certain situation for a short period of time, but if he stretches it for too long to make every decision of his life according to his past situations only, then he is no better than a fool. A fool knows that what he is doing is right. That is why we call him a fool. But who is bigger than a fool? The one who has survived a particularly bad situation and is scared to face another similar one. So he stops himself and keeps reminding himself of what all can go wrong in his life again.

This constant reminder that we start giving ourselves is what we need to stop doing immediately. As we remind ourselves of all the bad things that can happen to us again, the cosmos at large is also reminded of it again and again. And it will make sure that you face such a situation again and again – due to your own reminders. It will throw at you what you least want, but why? Because of your constant reminders which turn into fear and thus into reality. So be careful of what you think of and what you consciously remind yourself about when in certain situations. Catch those thoughts and ban them from entering your mind/thought process. No two situations can always be the same unless you want them to be. When they start being the same, you will realise that a pattern has started in your life because of what and why you think about certain things at certain times. Look carefully within your head, you shall find all answers within it.

## STOP MAKING PATTERNS

*Message given by Soloris*

There was a time when money in the hands of a few could turn the majority of men into futile and unsustainable morons. The years ended with nothing to spend but everything to hold and all to be loved. Let me explain in simpler words – in the times of kings and landlords, the rich people ruled. They never allowed the poor to stand on their own feet. They never let their share of fortune to be shared with anyone else. This hampered the growth of civilisation and also their own.

You are the connoisseur of what you make out of your life. As and how you start understanding what conscious thinking is, you will begin to realise how well you know yourself and how you do not need others to access yourself anymore. Once you know yourself fully, it is only you who will be able to make amends in your life. You will like the changes you make because of the efforts you put in to be the change. You will hold only yourself responsible and that you will be most proud of. Nothing that others may say should matter to you. What would matter most is how you think about yourself and how you change yourself to be at the highest level in your own eyes.

Leaps and bounds of energy is required in order to achieve what one sets himself/herself to achieve. This energy is at the highest when the idea of what you want is formulated. You think that everything can be possible and thus start thinking ahead, encountering all your problems with your solutions and then reaching the part where you have become a perfectionist. You dream of everyone admiring what you have achieved.

This pumped up energy starts to slow down the minute you actually encounter your very first problem or hurdle in your plan of action. The energy level that goes down is very little but this is the first indication of you having lesser energy and the (fleeting) thought of you not being able to achieve what you had set forth to achieve. Now my friends, the problem cannot be foreseen, yet we know that one or the other problem may arise when we are doing a task. So why get disappointed when it does arise or when it does take shape. You just need to make sure that you turn that problem into more energy rather than letting it deplete some of your energies.

Everyday, think of the many energies that you can gather together instead of feeling drained by each one of them. Feel the same excitement, the same feeling of being able to achieve the impossible that you had daydreamed about because that is exactly what you are getting my friend – the same kind of situations that may seem impossible to win over, but if you do, then you end up being a hero. Isn't that what you had dreamed of in the beginning? Well so now that you've got it, stop cribbing about it and get on with your big dream, your big idea, your big plan, because if you don't buckle yourself now then you won't have any energy left to complete your task. This is the main reason why most people cannot finish what they start because of the energy drain. Energy drains are also excuses that they make for themselves. It is the will power that is lacking. So if you've had at least 3-4 instances when you have not finished what you had started then you are making a pattern of your own misery. You need to be able to stop that pattern to set it straight. You just have to or it will start showing in your life, your relationships and your work. The rein is in your hands, my friend. So steer it where you want yourself to be steered (only after a lot of thought and consideration) or else you will soon find these reins being handed to this pattern and it will start steering you automatically. Save yourself when you have the time to.

Don't lose hope, don't lose energy; build it, work it up and you would have built yourself up.

In order to maintain high standards about anything what one needs primarily is to be focused in what one needs done. If the focus is lost then the task at hand is lost too. We sometimes like to lose focus because not dealing with it gives us more time to be careless and irresponsible. Nonetheless it weighs us down. The gravity of it makes us lose sleep and lose our energy for no particular reason. We delay our work so much that piling them all up in ourselves becomes a task in itself and so without realising this we feel unhealthy and dissatisfied with every aspect of the day.

To be able to change that, you need to have the focus along with the determination to go out to get all things started. You are the one in charge here; no one else is going to do it for you. Because even if someone did, the load is already registered in your body and since you didn't do it, the heaviness within you will still be there. So improve yourself to improve your health, your state of mind and your well being.

Don't lose your focus. Focus, Focus and Focus. Every day of the week, every week of the year and every year of your life. You should be fine, just fine.

## DO YOU KNOW *WHAT* YOU WANT?

*Message given by William*

Why is there no end to what we can't get? Why is the grass greener on the other side? Why don't we ever find ourselves in a situation of bliss all the time? After all even God would like to experience bliss. Why don't we choose a life and shower only good things on ourselves? Why don't we get what we want and also dictate how we should get it? The answer is simple; we have not yet reached the stage of understanding of how this universe ticks. How dreams become reality and how our thoughts and words are manifested and when we learn the art of what is called 'Conscious sub-conscious manifestation'. This art is simple. Think of what you want, do what you will as if you already had the 'thing' you wanted. You will always have what you wanted. If you don't get it, try and understand if there are any negative notions attached to the thing you want. You will find out clearly why you are not getting it. Ten out of 10 times you will find that your thoughts and actions are going in the opposite direction than the one necessary if you had the thing you wanted.

Very few people really understand that wanting something is not creating a manifestation nor is needing it badly. We need to be able to have an open heart to accept the things we need. It will be manifested in front of our eyes in the quickest timeframe. I always hear prayers such as – give me a big car or a big promotion or a big house, but simultaneously there are doubts in us that obstruct the need/readiness of the things we desire. How can God give you a big car when you have not decided which brand/model you want and you have conflicting thoughts such as, is it the right time for it, do I have enough money for it, have I really earned it, etc? Or should God give you the promotion when you yourself feel that you might not be ready for it?

'If there is a will there is a way', a very old but good saying. One of the most popular singers has sung these lines very beautifully. The expression is often associated with hard work, but it's hardly any work to know what you are willing to do, is there? If you truly want yourself to succeed at your workplace then no matter what your pay scale is at the moment, you do a good job. If you want another baby then no matter what, you will take the time to make plans for investing right and ensuring that you build your wealth.

Our manifestations need clarity of thought for them to take shape. If you want to buy a particular house then go all out and feel you are going to buy it today or tomorrow. You will see that you are living there in some time. It's very simple but not understood by most of us. How can you go on a vacation when you are troubled about your work, safety of the house, etc.? How can you save money when you truly want to buy all those accessories? How can you build your home when you feel incompetent doing it yourself? Asking anything from God will not help unless you are sure of what you truly want.

## THE ART OF ASKING WHAT YOU WANT

*Message given by Archangel Michael*

What you have been waiting for has been delivered to you and yet you are not ready to receive it. Why do you ask for it in the first place? Why do you have to think such thoughts when you know you will get what you have been asking for? What will you do to change how your life functions? We cannot make day into night and night into day for your convenience. You are asking for something that even you don't know you want or not.

*Message given by Soloris*

Soloris is my name and I can be seen all around you if only you look out for me. Any message that you get is sent through me or by me. I am your messenger, doing the delivery also at most times. So watch out for me. Ask me a question, a favour – that comes straight from your heart, for which you really want a solution and I shall help you with it.

Yet you need to also learn the art of asking first and then I will tell you about how you would receive the messages.

Let me explain with an example. A little boy wishes for a bike for his birthday but he gets something else. Now the intent of children is pure so where does the question of impure thoughts arise? It is not the lack of intent of the child that did not get him his bike but also the intent of his parents. Till the child is dependent on others, his thoughts, however pure, cannot fully claim what he wants. Because he is bound by the intents of the others as well as his own.

Now in the same case, had an adult wanted something and hadn't got it, he would need to understand that there is a valid reason behind it. An adult can always – firstly, earn it for himself, so he feels that only when I have earned for it, will I be able to buy it. Thus he puts a closure to his thought process of abundance there and then. He feels that he cannot ask for something if he cannot buy it himself. That is one limiting thought.

The solution is to ask for it whole-heartedly, without your logical mind doing the math for you of how and when and where. So, in order to control your logical mind, you need to stop and think without really having any thoughts. This can happen only during meditation. You go into such a deep concentration level that you yourself will come up with the reasons why you want or don't want anything. You will also be able to understand why it is important for you to want a particular thing just for the heck of getting it even when your heart is not into it. You will be able to listen clearly to your heart. The heart will give you all the reasons and solutions you are looking for.

Meditation provides a lot of answers to our every day problems. It helps us connect to our own selves from within, which can enable us to reach that state of peacefulness that our reasoning mind (not our logical mind) starts to work in a manner that provides us with all the solutions.

You will need to practice meditating daily to be able to taste what it is all about. You will need to put your mind to a short sleep while the other senses in you awaken and then your body will provide you with all the answers you need.

The next thing is to listen to the sounds of nature whenever you can. Separate the sounds of nature with the humdrum of the daily life to feel the peace and joy it fills you with. Do it for a few minutes, you will feel recharged with energy for the rest of the day. Nature has a beautiful way of reviving our energies. All we need to do is to just be aware of it. The smells, the sounds, the colours, the textures are so important. The most important being touch. We have forgotten what leaves, petals, stones, pebbles, barks and branches feel like. Get back to it, get back to nature on your knees to be able to touch and feel what we have forgotten. It will all love you back fully and without any anger that you have neglected it for so long. It will take you in its arms completely, lovingly, give you pure energies from itself.

Do this for ten days, then you will start to feel the difference in yourself. Being with nature is loving nature. When you love something that too is a way of meditating!!

I have been blessed to have this fine lad write whatever I tell him to, and this lad has me for everything else. I am all around him, in him. And you have your spirit guides around you as well. Speak with them, reach out to them. You will notice how your world changes.

You have you and you have your conscience. You and your conscience are currently two separate beings existing in you but you need to make them into 'One'.

With love of the light to you all

*— Soloris*

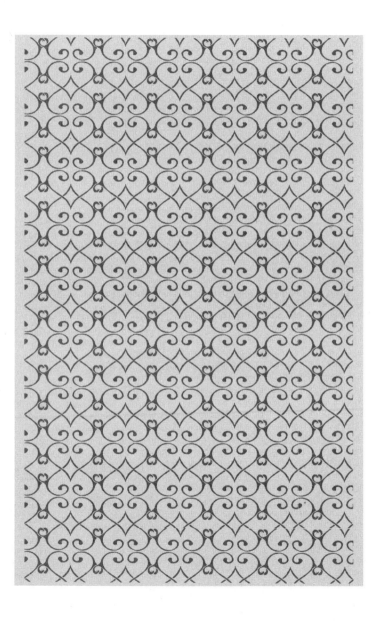

# 4

# The All Important Question: 'The Purpose of My Life'

*Message given by Soloris*

What I am about to embark on with you is a journey to the inner self. You would have by now realised that the path to the Lord or the Almighty is only one and is well treaded. Many have walked on it and many are walking on it. The question here is – when will you be walking that path? Well, to tell you simply and truthfully, if you are applying what you are currently reading then your inner journey to find the Lord has already begun.

It is not only for those who are fully aware of what they are doing but also for those who partially understand what they have to do.

The understanding is manifold. One can understand the formula yet not know why it is used or what it is used for. At the same time, many would know the use of a certain formula but not know how it was derived at in the first place. So there are different levels of understanding, none of which is incorrect or totally correct. Because there is always more that can be understood and therefore, experienced. So in order to broaden our understanding, one needs to stand underneath a tree full of leaves and branches then look at his problems from underneath. Many times problems can be solutions too. So everything about them should be unearthed.

Now, if you were to stand under a tree, how many leaves or branches do you think you could count? Branches are the many levels of understanding we have of the same issue/ problem/formula. The leaves are the many derivatives that come out from this understanding.

Can you confidently say that you have all answers or that you are looking at every aspect of the matter at hand? Surely not. It is only natural to not see it all from below. Because what about the branches that you can't see or what about the leaves right on top of the tree that can't be seen or counted? Well, these, my friend, denote the missing links to your understanding. Many things do exist that you cannot even imagine.

These are those levels; these are those leaves. Now in order to get to such high levels, you need to be able to trim the tree a bit. Bit by bit you will realise what is not necessary and whatever is not required. All that, which does not make too much sense or all the leaves that are limiting in nature – limiting your thought process – like many beliefs that you may have or a rigid mind set – all these levels or leaves need to be chopped down one by one. You will soon realise that you can after all see the top most branches and the top most leaves become visible for you to count. Now this tree you are looking at is a beautiful trimmed tree of a particular thought/problem/issue that exists in your life. Cross all levels and barriers and this tree (read-problem) will begin to vanish once you have seen and counted the last one of its leaves. Because then my friend, the issue or the problem will no longer be an issue as you would have moved on and the best solution is for the problem to not be a bother for you. Surpass all your problems in this manner. You would have planted this wonderful image of a tree in your mind and in your heart, so that it serves as a reminder of what and how to solve all your worries just by gaining the correct perspectives.

Half of them, you will realise, are just your assumptions and beliefs. Change these, make them go away, discard them like you would trim the unwanted leaves. All you would have left behind is a beautiful healthy looking tree, free from anything that can spoil it. The rotten leaves are never a part of you, you just happen to pick them up and attach them to yourself, knowingly or unknowingly. But now that you know, be careful about choosing what leaf you want to add to your tree – a healthy one or a rotten one? It's always your choice.

*Message given by William*

We are here to accomplish the tasks that we have set for ourselves before taking this shape. The moment we take shape, there are so many other distractions that make us forget why we have come here. Then, as and when we grow to a stage when we need to learn a particular lesson, situations get created to remind us of what we need to do. Some fear them and run away, some face them and fail and surrender yet there are some who pass with flying colours. We are all these three types in some aspect or the other.

Now what we need to think about hard and fast, are the aspects where we fall in the first two categories. Make a list, don't worry, the list won't be longer than 2–3 items. Even if it's long, you can class them in 2–3 main categories. Pick the one you find most difficult. Now concentrate on what all occasions you have suffered because you couldn't face that obstacle. How did people bring you discomfort by playing a role in that situation? Where does this situation occur the most? Add it to your list and for the next few days try and chart out a plan for yourself on how you should deal with this situation if it were to arise again.

When you are ready, go to those people and places with some excuse to be there and keep going there until you know you have overcome that obstacle completely. Until then you need to keep going back to them. Your plan of action on how to deal with these situations would automatically evolve, so give respect to each and every failed attempt. Once you have learnt one more dimension of the aspect you are destined to overcome, you should come out stronger than before.

You will be victorious if you follow the above; if not then there are other lifetimes to overcome them. Once your list is complete, you would then realise that new ones can be added. So my friend, don't feel bad about it. Rather think that you are overcoming your tasks for the next life as it will make you stronger than ever before. Weakness is a sign of creating strength. Losses are indications of what we will win. You are here is proof that you are going to be with Him.

When was the last time we told ourselves that we are fine to go on that extra mile? Is there any place we have wanted to go but could not as we fear what it might bring out in us? By not going to that place, you are blocking out the memories and energies of that place and time. The deep connection felt for articles, places and people is a source of inspiration and charging point for the soul. My friends, seek out what your heart is telling you. Answer the door leading to the satisfaction of your wishes and fulfilment. Go and reach out to the wondrous places of this world.

## A STORY

There was once a man who lived in a small hut near a mountain. He was a teacher to a group of small children. He was fond of his young wife, who really took good care of him. He was middle-aged and had got married recently. They could not have any children of their own. One day the man, after his class, goes down to the woods in search of a rabbit or a small deer for dinner. On his way he realises that his tools are not with him. To avoid going back, he picks up a stick to use as a weapon to attack the animals. While searching through the forest he sees a white rabbit and silently approaches it. However, he was not alone in chasing that animal. There was a fox eyeing the rabbit as well.

On realising that he wasn't alone in the pursuit, he quickly calculates the risk to his life if the fox came after him. While contemplating, he realises that he should go back as there are a lot of things waiting for him and resting on his shoulders and that he should not let it all go for this pursuit. The fox meanwhile aware of the man's presence tries not to get affected and show its own fear; ultimately, the two predators are so lost in their thoughts and fears that this allows the rabbit to escape. The rabbit goes into a hole that can't be accessed by any of them.

The man and fox are the fears in us to reach our goal. The man argued whether the goal was important enough and the fox was petrified to think anything. Thinking too much or too little when we face our fears leads us to miss the opportunity to make something out of nothing.

There are times when we don't want to do anything. We just take it easy and see how the world will tick if we do not participate in any activity. That feeling is coming out from the soul's need to access what we need to concentrate on. What is the first hurdle we need to leap over? So many things remain un-ticked and the list is getting too long. That is the time we feel lethargic and need time with ourselves to understand the priorities of our existence. In order to get the maximum from this phase, closely watch your surroundings. Take indications from the words being said by the people around you. Understand what you see amongst many different colours and shapes. If you (your attention) are getting stuck with a particular object then find out what it might signify, that is what your priority should be.

This phase of no action and introspection also happens when we have ticked all the boxes and don't know what to do next. So please welcome this phase, as it will help bring out the best in us. We need to observe and take cues from the universe around us. It will at least tell us that what we face today is not a matter of coincidence but an act of self-doing. Once we realise this important lesson, getting through any obstacle becomes easier to handle.

If you feel that you can't make out the pattern and symbols then reach out to your family and friends to ask for their help in determining your life's priority for the present time. If even they cannot understand, then there is nothing to worry about. You will see yourself coming back to this stage again and again until you find the way to understand what you need to determine.

The 'lesson' is very important to understand from the core of its existence till the end of its life span. The clearer the visions the faster we master them. The lesson of life is to understand what we are made of and what we need to do. Then we walk the path to reach what we originally charted as the 'destination'.

5

# How to Follow Your Heart

*Message given by Archangel Michael*

To go to a place or arrive at a particular destination, where our heart wants us to be, will be the best place to be. The mind is a tool that is most often misused and regularly abused. This tool is for finding ways to get things done and not a tool to decide what we should be doing. It is an important part of the soul's journey to understand the importance and the limitation it possesses. It can see black and white, like the super computers. The binary language is all that they are capable of understanding, no matter how elaborate the programme is.

The more we discover the limitations of the mind the more we rely on our awareness and our innate nature to follow what the heart says. 'Heart', or you can also say the soul; will always guide you to the right direction. You need to believe and not doubt. Then you would be able to do what is necessary for you in that moment in time. The mind will be covered in a separate book that will be written by these authors. However, for the time being, we just need to understand that logic and rules of the game are understood so cleverly by the mind that it does not allow the soul to experience love and hate, wealth and poverty. The mind will need to be utilised when we are extremely sure in understanding what we are here for and what we need to do.

Where would we be if we only allowed our brains to tell us where to go and what to do? You would think somewhere good certainly, as then there would be no self-interest or selfishness and our constant need to tell ourselves that it is for our own good. What will happen if this does not come true? If we were to get stranded? In fear of all these situations we would choose the least risky and least fun place to be in, won't we?

*Message given by Soloris*

Now we come to the moment of truth. Not the truth that can be deciphered by mere machines, but our own truth, which we ourselves most times fail to recognise. There is a very fast and easy way to determine if we are saying the truth or not.

Now the trick is to ask a question to yourself and give both (yes and no) answers after a lot of thought or even without any thought. Your answers will either be a 'yes' or a 'no'. Now as soon as you answer either one, notice how your heart feels and how it has reacted. If it feels heavy and has a feeling that something is unfinished or not satisfactory, then that would mean that you have lied to yourself. However – if the answer you say or think of gives you full satisfaction and your heart feels at peace without any upheavals – then that is the truth that you have discovered about yourself. So if next time you are stuck in a tricky situation and you really don't mean what you are saying, then you will be able to feel the same in your heart. It is then up to you to rectify the situation and do what you should be doing in the correct fashion. This is a very easy yet strong tool to understand how you yourself feel about a given situation. Your body/heart will never lie to you so you can have full faith and trust that the way your heart feels is the way to go!

You can try this even right now. Think of anything that you already know is true about yourself and then give a positive and a negative answer to your question. Do this a few times, so that you are able to properly read your heart. Once you are able to read your heart, it will be a very peaceful and beautiful life that you will lead, which will not have any confusion or misunderstandings, at least from your side.

## HOW 'LUCK' WORKS

*Message given by Archangel Michael*

For a lucky person things happen seamlessly, for an unlucky person it's hard work and hard work only. Little or no results are seen at the end of the day. So doesn't this mean that the person is indeed 'lucky' as he/she is closer to God or has committed less sins as compared to the unlucky one? The truth really is that the lucky one has either overcome the lesson, which the unlucky one is finding difficult to cope with, or the lucky one has yet not reached that stage of awareness to work on that particular aspect. Rather he/she have their own set of priorities which are necessary for them to reach the stage of understanding this aspect.

Luck is a sequential activity. It broadly works on the same concept of following what your heart says, that is having no doubt that anything will ever come in the way of achieving one's dream.

In order to understand what we want to do, we all need to listen to our hearts. Once we know what we want to do, how do we achieve it? Two things are necessary for one to accomplish what the heart says. To have full faith that the thing we seek is good and pure and is for the benefit of everyone. If there is any doubt then it may never happen due to conflicting thoughts and manifestations. So first we need to believe that what we want to do is the best thing to do.

The second thing is to remind ourselves to keep walking until we get there. Not everyone will start and finish the same day. Sometimes it takes years to reach. Remember even if we were able to reach one milestone, we would have given one more dimension to the source. So let it take time, just keep reminding yourself of what and where you need to be.

At a concept level the above would make sense; however when we apply this rule to our day to day lives we can't follow this without having numerous questions about whether I am doing it right, or the way/path I choose may not be correct at all. My dear friends, believe in what you choose for yourself, as it cannot be half as bad as what the world has been asking us to do. Go all out to achieve your goals.

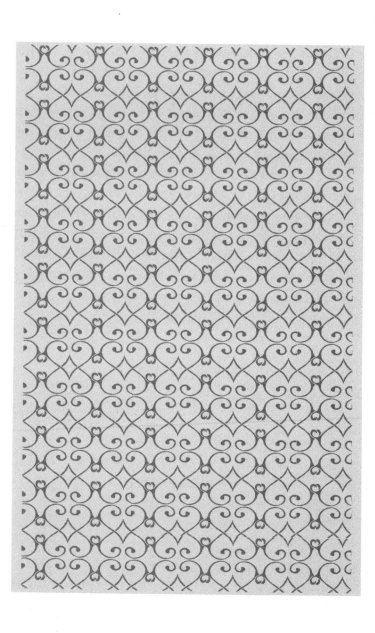

# 6

# The People in My Life

*Message given by William*

A 'family' is getting together of a pattern, a maze that a group of souls choose, so that their learnings can grow manifold. People in the family will either be good, bad or insignificant in having any impact on one's life. The ones who have a good impact are our enemies as they hinder the process of learning. They are always trying to keep you away from the root cause of an issue and are finding ways to distract you from the purpose of your life. Now this may sound wrong and there is no reason to have less love and respect for them but realise that you don't need to go to them for shelter each time you face a difficult situation. You don't need to understand the purpose of their lives, just concentrate on yours.

Now the second category of people, the problem makers, the bullies, the ones we feel are causing us most pain and unhappiness, these people are your true friends. They are here to teach you what you truly need to learn and experience in order to fulfil your destiny. I am always surrounded by those souls, that have passed over, who have such a lot of love for these 'bad influences' that it is difficult to put it all on paper. The bad influencer will make you feel you are unworthy, so 'you' need to find out why you are worthy and when you know your own worthiness there is nothing that can make you feel unworthy again. The bad influencer may *tell* you to go away from them, for you to realise the importance they have in your life. The aspect you miss the most, is what you need to find within yourself. The bad influencer can be beside you to support, by not supporting you in your decision, because they want you to be confident of what you truly want. Then you will not need anybody's approval for anything.

Lastly, the third kind, the insignificant ones. Well, they truly are the most significant ones to watch out for. They closely resemble what you are; they are your examples of do-s and don't-s. They are your real teachers. Your 'bad influencers' often become insignificant when you distance yourself from them. But a distance of a kilometre, a mile, intercity, inter country has no real bearing when we realise that galaxies and planets are so well connected. Allow feelings for these people to surface; we need to understand their purpose in our life so as to be able to really grow out of any insignificant understanding or issue. The world will change in front of us if we looked at these three kinds of people in true light i.e. with the true understanding of what they truly are for us and for our growth.

The family members are all in the same soul group. The group is always complete in itself but they need all the people in the group to step up and be as perfect in the qualities that each individual in that group contains.

Look at the people around you, see why you like being among them, what qualities attract you to them. What is that you always wanted to do and never had the courage to do? Take notice of your wife/husband. Why you chose him or her to be your life partner? He/she is fulfilling a very big part of what you always wanted to do. They complete you in that aspect. Once you have realised that aspect, you need to take that and make it your own. Once you have mastered that art, you will have completed a major part of your destiny.

Now let's reverse the story. What is that aspect you don't like about your partner? You have hundreds of fights going through similar arguments again and again. You can't seem to find any answer why he/she behaves in the manner that they do. Now take the behaviour and ask yourself why does it bother you? Why is this person making you realise that something is amiss? You need to get answers from within and you need to be able to tell yourself if that aspect in you is finding it difficult to cope with.

It has nothing to do with anything or anybody else; it is your issue. If you are able to realise this, then you will master what 99.8 per cent people are not able to in one lifetime. Your partner is the best teacher you would have ever got. Your partner will always show you the path of freedom from any sort of confinement. Your partner will help you even if you don't care. Work upon yourself. You, 'yes, you' are capable of reaching your goal if only you take notice of why and what you need to learn from your partner. The best part is that God has given us numerous opportunities to be able to discover this.

The day you find out that people around you are there for a reason and you start taking notice of who and why, you will be on top of the world. You will see exactly why you are feeling bad and getting stuck. You wouldn't ever need to go to a friend or foe to remind yourself what is lacking in your life.

★

A crying child asks for attention. A beggar asks for money. A businessman asks for money and time. A teacher asks for undivided attention and focus. A parent asks for love. A policeman asks for obedience. There is a need, which must be fulfilled for every individual. However, we are here to focus on our needs and not that of others.

As a child, my need is to get attention and I ask for it from my parents. The parent is looking for love, hence is always giving attention – both are fulfilling each other's needs. This is natural but only if you concentrate on your own need rather than the need of others. You need to do everything that will satisfy your need.

We don't need to work hard to meet others' expectations. The design of our lives has been made such that we will only meet people with whom our needs will be met. By not understanding this design we often neglect our own selves to fulfil the needs of others. All we need to do is focus only on our own need and we can never go wrong.

Don't think that this rule would change in different situations. Even in a disastrous situation this rule will work. So, my friends, focus on what you need and you will reap all the rewards there are to be reaped in this lifetime.

## SOULMATE

In our lives there is always one person who has left a mark or a scar on our souls. Can you recall one such person? He or she may be insignificant now but that person in the little time they were with you, made you realise a very important aspect about yourself. These beings are your soulmates. Now isn't this a heart breaker? Why wouldn't our soulmate live with us, why would they just come and go? If you were truly listening to what I have previously said, you wouldn't argue. Soulmates are our help line, our blood bank, our need to ensure we are always reminded of what we truly are, to do what is necessary for us to reach our soul's destiny. Their presence has such an impact that even minutes with them may seem like years. They can give you so much insight about yourself that you don't need any other help. My friends, our soulmate gives us the dimension of the boundary we need to cross, they give us exactly what is necessary for us to know about ourselves. When you meet your soulmate, there is an instant connection, which may not always be positive. At times when you talk to and get to know your soulmate, you feel elevated, on top of this world. When they leave you, you realise their importance even more. But what we truly need to remember is the time we spent with them. What they felt about us may have sounded ridiculous at the time, but it starts making sense in due course of time. Always remember what they told you about 'you'.

Not all people experience the company of soul mates. The few who do, need to reread this chapter a few times to be able to grasp what has been said.

# 7

# Love

*Messages given by Archangel Michael, Soloris and William*

The love in your lives comes to some of you easily but for most it happens very rarely. Some are loved since childhood and some during married life. But sometimes any kind of love is not enough. You still lack something. And here is what it is – the love for yourself. Most people go on with their lives giving up things/aspirations or living according to the needs and wants of others. You take it for granted that you don't have time for yourselves. You even forget to drink water or to put food in your mouth because you are busy feeding others or too busy attending meetings or clearing mails to even take a quick bite. This is not love of self. Everyone needs to learn to love themselves but at the same time remember not to spoil themselves rotten. And how might one do that? It is the addictions you make for yourselves that you think would keep you going. You indulge so much into them that you forget that instead of loving yourself – you are doing just the opposite.

It takes guts to be able to get out of any kind of an addiction. And it is not that easy – however small or big, mostly everyone has some kind of an addiction. Find out what yours is and chalk out a plan to erase it/normalise it/ balance it. Do remember, for you to get over an addiction you do not need to replace it with another addiction.

Now love comes to us sometimes naturally and sometimes it is imposed on us. Like in an arranged marriage. You will love your spouse one day or the other, sooner or later because now you are married to him/her. Love is good, natural or imposed. Love makes you smile; it makes your world look brighter and prettier. But what happens when you are in so much love that it begins to become claustrophobic for you? You are always thinking of the wellness of the person you love. You are always worried about him/her. You keep regular tabs on them. You make sure that you show them enough love so that they don't feel that you don't love them enough. You have to go out of your way to change some aspects of your life/your habits and stop being who you are in order to fulfil this 'love'. It is all good for sometime but most times you take 'compromise' as a way of loving each other a given. As if compromise needs to come with love. You get love and compromise comes with it for free!

Well, this is the story with each one of you and it is not bad until this love starts to make you so claustrophobic it drains away your energy to love. This is when 'hate' sneaks in. Sometimes it gets so strong that it even has the ability to push two people away from each other's lives completely. Love happens when the hearts are fresh and uncluttered but you clutter your hearts with all the worrying and dramas that you create for yourselves and your loved ones.

Take for example: parents and children. The parents are so worried about their children's routine that they always hurry things up. If anything goes off routine they don't like it because then the next day's routine would be broken. They are so worried about 'tomorrow' that they just waste 'today' in disciplining and shouting to hurry everything. Instead of enjoying the little tasks with their children, they just speed things up and remain in a really foul mood most of the time. If one single thing goes wrong the parent will blame the child for disrupting the routine for the entire day – this happens almost everyday.

This is claustrophobia. You need to catch yourself in the act to stop right there. Take it easy. Relax. The routine is not you. You have made it up. Maybe you made it thinking it would be best for you and your loved ones. So why does it not feel so joyful everyday? Think about it. Understand your and the other person/child's limitations. Realise that you need to be full of fun and joy. Include fun and joy as part of your routine.

Insecurities arise when you love someone too much – especially in the case of mothers and their children or even between couples. They arise from not having faith in:

1.  Yourself – you are not enough for your children/loved one and because of you the other would suffer or grow apart.
2.  Your loved ones – because they cannot take proper care of themselves and cannot carry the responsibilities they ought to.
3.  In God/Source/Universe – that it would not help your loved ones in their hour of need. As if the universe was greedy or pricey enough to take care of only those who prayed to be taken care of. No, the universe is at your service. Always. Even when you are not asking from it. If you have faith that the universe is taking care of your loved ones at all times you would never even need to pray because when you believe, what you believe in, happens.

If you fear losing a loved one then you need to spend time with them. Give them love and support. And you'll understand why the feeling of insecurity was coming to you.

And how would giving them love and support make one understand one's insecurity? The answer is very simple. If you love someone with the fear of losing them then you know that you need to work on the insecurity. If you love out of unconditional love and nothing else then you don't have any reason to fear. Love and fear are two opposite feelings; however we consider them extensions of one another. For example, 'I love my son so much that I fear what will happen if I lose him'. You don't need to over protect anybody or keep them in confinement or isolation. We need to do what is necessary (an absolute must) in a situation we want to happen.

The way we give love is important for us to understand whether it is because of love or fear. Mind you, in close relationships there could be both. We just need to deal with the insecurity and the fear will go away.

The fear has nothing to do with love. NOTHING. Fear blocks love and well-being. Take out fear to be filled with an abundance of love.

People often have a fear of darkness or heights. To overcome that, speak to people and read about the people who have overcome this fear. You could always be led in the direction where you find the key to overcome your fear.

## THE JOURNEY TO LOVE

*Message given by Soloris*

We are all bound together by the Akashik records. We are all a part of one another. We are all integrated together in the most sublime form. Why do the rich feel they have nothing to do with the poor? Why do the poor feel they cannot get rich?

It is these feelings precisely that are created for us all, especially, so we can learn from these thoughts and these feelings. Every emotion is circular. It has a start and an end but it still keeps going round and round till we find out for ourselves that there really is no end and thus we form a loop of that same emotion.

Can you think of an emotion beyond love? Once you can see every emotion with love, you will have no further thoughts of any other emotion. The circle is complete once love comes into the picture. Use it in an example, an everyday emotion that you have. Use the above and try the above. Get love in your thoughts, find something nice in that particular emotion and feel the loop trying to complete itself. It will work, it always does. Love can get you anywhere; you just have to think it.

## LOVE IS FOREVER

*Message given by William*

Once you love somebody, you can never un-love them. No matter what. Because when love enters your heart, it enters to stay. It does not know how to leave. So there is no need to be insecure about whether someone loves you or not even if they stop seeing you or telling you every day. You may grow apart but that does not mean that at that moment when you had loved – it wasn't love. So whenever you love someone, they will always hold a very special place reserved just for them in your heart.

You might think you love a person wholeheartedly but there are bits and pieces of your heart that always belong to more than just one.

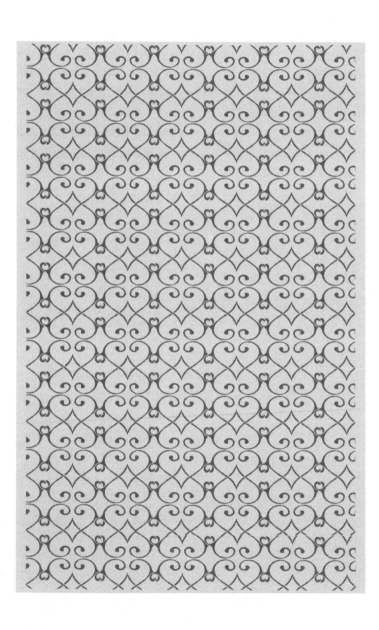

# 8

# Catch Your Thoughts

*Message given by Soloris*

We consider each and every step in this fast pace life of ours but why not the same thought when we are choosing our thoughts? Why are we so casual with what we think? Just because we can? Or just because nobody else can read them?

It is one thing that we have in secret, in hiding from another – our thoughts. But what we don't understand is that it is our thoughts that our body stores as images, pictures, words, sentences and sounds. This body of ours can resurrect itself from just one cell, again and again and again. In that one cell, we store all our thoughts and all our actions that we have thought of or done until now – the present moment. The body has a habit of allowing these thoughts, from many previous years of lifetimes, to turn into actions. So if you are witnessing your life and are unable to understand why certain situations occur when you could never even imagine them, it is your thoughts and actions from your previous lifetimes that are unfolding in front of you. These situations happen to be the dialogues between you (in the present) and your past. Your past is always staring at your face. You just don't acknowledge it most of the time (99 per cent).

In order to be able to catch your past, you need to be very strict with your thoughts first. You need to make sure that none of your thoughts create more troublesome situations for you in the future. Once you have mastery over your thoughts, you will be able to identify situations that trigger those thoughts that come back again and again to haunt you.

In this case now, you will need to find the perfect way of dealing with your thoughts, so it will be best for you to face the same kind of situations, again and again and again. These situations will be like a practice ground where you can try out new thoughts that work for you. I know it is not easy to put yourself in such situations. Yet in the larger picture you really are making a big difference to your self-healing process.

Once you have found the thought process that works for you in a similar kind of a situation, you will realise that you have moved on. Now those situations will no more be a bother for you. Then you can move on to another situation that bothers you.

Start with the little situations of life, your daily routine, the traffic on your way to work, the vegetable sellers, the milkman, the morning routine. Anything. Just pick up one single thing that bugs you the most everyday or most days. The change will be a gradual one but don't lose hope or patience. Just work on it everyday and it will slowly and steadily take place of the original thought.

*Message given by Archangel Michael*

The focus we have on the project we are doing at the moment, determines if it will be successful or not. The focus to complete it, to get it right and to ensure you get the right and effective results at the end of the day. Now apply the same thing on the issue which is persistent in your life. The Fishbone Analysis* would reveal the various factors contributing in making the issue dominant in our life. All those factors indicating that they are the source of the problem. However, which amongst them is the main one to go after? Just pick one of them and ask yourself – why is this here? Is it telling me something? Is there anything else that it is trying to bring to my attention? What can be done to be better prepared for this particular aspect of the issue? Prepare for yourself a full action plan to achieve or withstand the next occurrence. The more focussed

---

*Fishbone Analysis also known as the cause and effect analysis and is done to identify potential factors causing an overall effect.

you are, the easier it will get for you to create an experience of overcoming that part of the issue. If you do it and experience a 100 per cent success on that part, I can assure you that you will be completely ready to automatically deal with all the other factors adding to the main issue. Try it and remember to focus.

The scrapbook of our life seems to be full of moments that we like to cherish and smile at but what exact meaning do our special moments hold? The times when we are the happiest and the times when we are the saddest are the memorable moments of our lives. The other moments are not of much value. They are the mundane things of our lives. The routine, as we call it. They are not memorable and neither are they worth remembering because they have become a part of us – our second nature. So when we are sad or happy, it is not a part of our routine life but something out of the ordinary. These moments, we feel, define ourselves but actually they don't. The other moments, the everyday hustle bustle, are what we should be concentrating on. Are we being good to the car driver who is honking the horn from the back while going to the office? Are we really saving a lot by arguing unnecessarily with the vegetable vendor? Are we really following the rules laid by the cops or the government? Are we not keeping quiet about matters that should be shouted about? Are we not being lazy in doing what we should be doing for our body? Are we being responsible enough for our parents, our family, our neighbours, our friends? Are we giving ourselves enough attention? Or maybe more attention than is required?

These above are the general thoughts that should become second nature to us. What we follow – routine – is not something to be taken for granted. However, it is something that can bring to us the thought process we require to change our reactions towards our everyday life. Don't just react because it's happening; tackle it in a different manner, in a more positive fashion and you will start liking yourself better and better. In the happy and sad situations – you know how you are to react. It is the everyday situations that you need to be perfect at.

*Message given by Soloris*

Our routine also includes what we wear everyday. So, why do we wear clothes that make us look what we are not? Clothes so tight that the skin cannot breathe. So dark that the skin cannot get any colour or light. In earlier times, for women to have the perfect waistline and bust, they were strapped and pulled so hard that the body took the shape of the clothes whereas it should have been be the other way round.

Don't hide your body. Let it be free.

Whatever one finds himself most comfortable in should be worn. It is not that our thinking propels such thoughts but the thoughts of others around us and the ones we have grown up with. Break those thoughts and barriers. You will realise that there is no such thing as a healthy or an unhealthy style of dressing.

## FROM THOUGHTS TO MANIFESTATIONS

Here we are sitting in the comforts of our houses, reading the newspaper and feeling bad about the not so fortunate ones everyday. But is it all? Is it enough for us to not do anything but sympathize from a place where nobody will hear; from a place where nobody can know?

You can change that and here's how – in order to be able to help the ones who are in need, you will need to formulate a thought that is very precise in what you want. Think that thought over in your head. Once you have worded/formed the perfect thought (of what you want said/done) you can speak it out loud and speak it with conviction and feelings. As many people do this, the people who require help will get it in the most magical of ways from the universe through you. Send them thoughts and they will receive what you want given to them. However, do realise that your negative thoughts will only work negatively for you and not for others.

I shall explain – when anything negative comes out from you – thought, action or word, you create cracks around your well-being, around your aura. Positive thoughts fill these cracks and negative thoughts will only broaden these cracks. Anyone wanting to harm you cannot because only you can harm yourself. If you are happy then you are happy because no one else can make you happy. Think about it.

You want something and when you get it, you are happy. But who wanted that 'something' in the first place? You. So whenever you create a want for yourself, you yourself are making a way for you to be either happy or not happy.

Whenever you are sad, you can face yourself in front of the mirror and find out what you had wanted that has made you sad. Being sad is not at all a bad thing. It makes you appreciate when you are happy. Sad is not at all bad because it shows you how strong you can be. Sometimes you give in to a way of life (life style) too much and when it is taken away from you, you realise that you could do without so much stuff. You need to feel sad from time to time in order to un-clutter your life. It is like throwing trash out or giving away stuff that you don't need anymore. Once the sadness is over, you realise how calm and clean you have become. It is just a refreshing emotion for your body – sadness.

Yes, you will not feel this greatness when you are being sad. Maybe not the first few times you are sad but you will start noticing the 'un-clutteredness' eventually. Believe me, you will start appreciating it, too.

*Message given by William*

It's quite essential to be safe and secure. To be in a position to protect ourselves from the common fears like burglary, sins of flesh and protecting our property. The reason is that you and you alone can have a secure thought process.

However, society and people living with you will bring in thoughts which may bring in doubts that may get stuck in you subconscious or conscious mind. The doubts and fears may manifest something untoward. So my dear friends, do what earthly common sense tells you to do and yet fight all thoughts which are not necessary – that obstruct the path to your destiny.

You have been good so far since you have taken the shape of your existence in this world as a 'conscious human'. The journey now is going to evolve a lot of introspection, a constant will and determination to follow your heart's need. To fight away distractions and disturbances that come in your way. Those of you who have read the book so far need to understand what will help them in staying focussed in their path rather than thinking I was better off being ignorant about the game of life. If you wonder and see any benefit of going back, then just concentrate and really think through about how much and how long will the benefit of being ignorant last successfully.

# 9

# Your Body Is Beautiful...
# Listen to It!

*Message given by William*

The past between you and your soul is carried in your body.
Look at your body to find out how nice or not so nice you
have been so far on your journey on earth. The ailments,
weaknesses and the strengths from the past have made you
what and who you are at present. The outer looks never
determine your journey. Only you know your body well –
not your doctor, not your spouse, not your mother – no one

else. Just you. You will know if you are going to fall sick or what parts of your body are weak.

You can interact with your body just like you do with your doctors or even friends. You can let your body know to be prepared for times when you know you will be stressed or times when you know you will be neglecting it for a reason. Communicate and your body will reply. Start tuning-in to what your body wants from you. Don't feel that you know more about your body than your body itself. It (your body) will tell you more than anyone else can. Your body will heal itself if and when required, whenever you tell it to. It will discard away all that you tell it to.

Be truthful to your body because your body is always true to you. Listen to your heartbeat. It beats at a rhythm. Have you ever just put your hand on your chest and connected with your heart. Everyday send loving emotions and soothing and healing thoughts to your entire body. Your body loves you, only you don't know it most of the times. Show your body that you love it too. Enjoy the harmony of being one with yourself and see how your worries about your health decrease and then disappear.

★

There are times when we feel weak and lethargic. Those are good times for our body because it is the body's way of telling us that we need to slow down a bit and take care of the body. Eat well, sleep well and most of all rest well. The body requires all these things to function well. If any one is not met with properly, the body refuses to function at its normal pace. We have all gone through these stages but how many times have you actually given your body what it really requires? For some, it may need to be exercised, for some the body may need a break from the routine and for some the body may just require proper rest. If you think about it, these are not very difficult things to do. To exercise – you don't need to go to the gym. Start with your housework; get all the pending work done. Your body will feel energized after accomplishing the tasks that have been waiting for so long. The mind too will feel light and clear of the burden you did not realise it was carrying.

Exercising can also mean – play and fun! So jump around like a child or play, dance with your child or partner. Do something adventurous at your nearby adventure park. Run around, go for a refreshing swim, play hide-and-seek. Anything new that you have not done for a while. Pick up the household, do some extra cleaning. Anything that makes your body move in positions that it normally does not move in, is exercise!

If you are feeling weak and exhausted then take time out to just sit back and listen to some good music or read a book or a magazine. Don't let your mind be occupied by stupid games on the phone or the video games. Your mind will tire and so will you. They don't provide any stress release, in fact just the opposite.

Being all by yourself is also another way to unwind. Let yourself into a train of (pleasant) thoughts or just daydream while lying down.

You may argue with yourself or with what you are reading and say – I don't have enough time to sit and do nothing. But you know that in the 24 hours given to you and to each one of you, you do have the time to relax and unwind. You know it somewhere back in your head. You only fail to face it and acknowledge it. This is your conscience. This is what you need to face. This is who you are. You can run away from it for a time but not forever. It will catch up so don't hide from it. This is what this book is all about. Making you aware of what you already know deep down and making you realise that what you know is true because you and many others like you are reading what is true. Now, once you have read this, there is no going back on what you know. It gets all imprinted in your conscience and that is what your purpose is. Listen to it and follow it.

Love to you all in your journey of finding your conscience!

# 10

# Tapping Your Reservoirs

*Message given by William*

Centuries ago we saw the birth of a beast, a human in shape of an animal. It was called a werewolf. People saw it change from an animal to a human and vice versa. That creature was very gentle as it knew the power it possessed. The very thought of intellect of a human and the agility of a beast is so compelling to our mind that we started fearing these creatures and resisting their growth.

The werewolves and the other creatures that are a mix of the human and animal form possess great endurance. Their bodies can adapt to changes in surroundings much better than humans. They can live in extreme climatic conditions.

What we need in this world are people like those who could defend the human race from all the harmful technology and their side effects. They can show a path to all humans that technology alone cannot give happiness. Nature is very vast and abundant and these days we miss the happiness of nature. Living a life of a lion can be so powerful that no king or politician in human form can enjoy such power. If they could interact with humans and explain the beauty of their land then this world would be much fuller than it currently is.

What we need now is nearly obsolete. There are a few creatures out there but they have lost belief that they were here to bring harmony to the world when chaos prevailed. Many don't even need to convert from one form to the other, as they are content to take one side only.

Ok, why does this feature in this book? The only reason is that we need to tell ourselves of the power we have in our reservoirs. We have them in our blood and veins. The human body shape has come after we have taken births as a tiger, elephant, monkey, whale, a dinosaur, etc. So we can regenerate the power we once had in ourselves if we ever need to.

The belief that we can and the constant reminder to ourselves can bring forth all our buried talents. What you can do today is a consolidated summary of all your past feats. However, beauty is in the details. We need to be able to understand each strand of our multi-faceted talents to unearth what our true potential is. So 'you', yes you, will be a singer if you can find your roots back to a life when you rehearsed to achieve a beautiful voice and rhythm. Tapping of our past talents is not necessary to achieve the purpose of our lives. But tapping them can lead to accomplishing much more than what you originally came here for. Remember the ticking off rule.

So how can I unearth a talent that I don't know even exists. Well ask yourself, what is it that you felt is like a super power that you always wanted to display. The person writing this wanted to sing in front of a huge audience. He wanted to be like the most sensational music icon. However, ask his wife how off tune he currently is. For him to unearth what he is truly missing is to relive the many events in at least 25 of his previous births, where he practised music as a way of life. One life after another he increased his expertise in the art form and now in this present life, he doesn't need it. So *he* chose not to be linked with music in this life. However, this doesn't mean that he can't return. He can, most definitely, by the time he is retiring from an active work life; he will find his solace in music. But for that he first needs to finish writing this book and many others to accomplish what he set out to achieve in this life.

You can unravel your lost talents through Past Life Regression.

[Past Life Regression can be best understood by reading *Many Lives, Many Masters* by Dr Brian Weiss.]

I wish you all the very best.

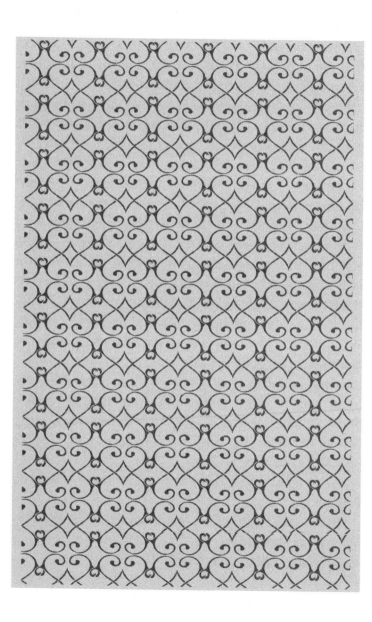

# 11

# Change the Little Things

*Message given by William*

## OUR HABITS

This book is regarding many things. Things that you may have come across in your day-to-day life, yet you don't feel are important enough to dwell upon or to ponder on. Why do we have a habit to overlook the smallest of our habits that do not interest us as well?

Why do we develop them to such an extent, that the habits become us? We start to feel that we were not who created our habits but our habits are a part and parcel of who we really are. So, we really were born with our mind, body and soul plus our habits. Our habits, we feel, are our bonus! Whether good or bad, they make you.

What if a person did not have any habits? It would simply mean that every time he saw situations in a different manner, from a different angle and every time he reacted differently. Take for example that a man has to run to his office everyday to keep up with his overweight problem. Now he has made it a habit to run to his office everyday, no matter what. Yet what if he had no habits at all?! He would run to the office, ride a cycle, drive a car, walk to the office, eat less in the first place or join a gym to lose his fat.

The amount of options a person has, when not part of habits, makes him realise what mistakes he had been making and how he was limiting his own thoughts and beliefs. This will also make him recognise the inner confidence in him of breaking old habits to rebuild them spontaneously. His reflexes will get stronger – as a result every situation he faces will be dealt with differently, not with a closed mind.

## OUR EGO

It is also important to give your ego a boost from time to time. However, this needs special care and attention, because the wrong kind of boost will only end up harming the ego.

What you can do is stack a set of cards on a table to

make a pyramid and realise for yourself how far up ahead you are from the others around you. Now start to feel how the ones around you may be feeling at their own positions. Your job is now to bring everyone up to your position, in the best possible manner you can manage. If you cannot do something directly, send them happy and encouraging thoughts everyday. Once they begin to grow, you will yourself realise how much more you have grown. This is a beautiful way to keep your ego happy and content. You will be happy when your friends/colleagues grow because you have also had a hand in making them grow. The atmosphere around you will change and just by thinking well, all will be well, for you as well as for all those around you.

## OUR SLEEP

Why wake up when you can sleep on? A question many may have thought of but not considered answering. The sleep technology is such that when it comes, it comes beautifully but when it is forced upon, it will only create negative results in you. Take for example – a girl sleeping a fitful sleep at night and waking up fresh in the morning. Yet, since she can sleep a little longer, she takes the opportunity to sleep on. Now, this extra bit of sleep she has taken will be full of dreams and various thoughts. When she does finally wake up she will be full of guilt for not doing all she had wished to complete the previous day. She would not feel fresh and well rested, even though she should.

Now the question here is, should she stop feeling guilty over a period of time and become indifferent towards her own attitude regarding her sleeping habits? Well, once she realises what she is doing, she needs to be able to change the habit. That's it. No one or nothing can help. If she does not then she will have to bear the brunt of it in the next or the coming lifetimes.

So why burden yourself with such trivial things. Carry a clean slate to the next life so it is smooth sailing for you. For nobody else, but yourself. Think about it!

# 12

# The Complete Journey

*Message given by William*

We take the shape of our ancestors to remind ourselves of what we were. We constantly need reminders of what we came here to achieve. All the un-fought and lost battles need to be brought out again as we need to understand our own game plan to overcome each weakness, each sorrow and each agony that could not be overcome.

We will continue to take form as a beggar until we learn to share our food and clothing. We will always be fat until we understand why it is important to have food. Why food can give us so much love and affection for ourselves. Why we can be so full of ourselves that we can't take anything else that can make us full.

Yes, I am a soul who is writing through this person and I am wilfully making my friend's hand move in the direction I want it to move to tell you, 'Yes, you', that it is possible to get out of any routine, any *aadat* (habit), any fascinations, any sorrow if we know what is causing us to behave in the manner we are behaving.

## DEATH

I am very fond of people who say I am going to die very early. It's because they feel lonely without us. However, we really don't want people to die and come to us early. We just want to be around when they do come.

I am very happy to see when the world agrees on a particular topic. It's great when people accept that we have to go (die) after all. But does one wonder why and what led people to believe this myth?

Earlier, 10,000 years was the average age of people. Before Christ, they lived and lived and only passed on, on free will, as they wanted to change their bodies. We started to see the change as an end and started fearing what we ourselves were choosing for ourselves. Why don't we live longer now? Because we can't break the very core thought that we will ultimately die. If one truly believes that one can live on, then he/she is considered mad and faces people's condemnation. So, why should I believe what is correct? I will only believe what sounds correct to most of us. The angels guarantee that if you keep children in an area free from all thoughts of death, they will reach 10,000 years.

## THE JOURNEY BACK

'We are all here to learn a lesson'. Now, haven't we heard that before? Yes, it is true and we can't change that. However it is not one lesson, it's a series of lessons. From one to the other and then another. So are we so foolish or is there no end? Well, there is an end – God.

How many Gods have lived on the earth plane or are living? Very few. To be God, it takes a lot of learning and practice. Being close to being HIM is spectacular; however reaching the stage is extraordinary. Can you, 'Yes, you', reach that state in one lifetime?

I think so but the important question is, 'Do *you* believe so?' We have so much trouble getting used to regular things (things that majority of the people think are regular or routine) that it takes so much unlearning to do and so we feel its never ending.

It's not easy to become GOD. It is possible because we have to ultimately go in that direction. We have to be steady and ready to allow the forces of the universe to show us the path towards HIM. We do not have to do anything that will be termed as extraordinary to achieve HIS state. We will be there by doing/undoing regular things (regular meaning day-to-day chores). We have been given a human form, as that's the closest to Him. We are superior beings and are going to act in a manner so that we maintain our superiority.

We all came from Him and have lost our way back. We need to solve the puzzles, bridge the gaps, make way and find the path to go back to Him.

There are times when we are nowhere, neither on the earth plane nor in the l-b-l (life before life) state. We are in union with a power generator, 'The Source', to recharge ourselves. We sleep and when we are in a deep slumber we connect our cords to the source to recharge what is about to die or needs to be revived. This process is so subtle that very few realise that this even happens. Well, sleep does make one relaxed. The lack and overdose of sleep causes us to function in a less than optimised manner.

Lack means the process is not given enough time and overdose means that the areas covered are so relaxed that too much inertia sets in for them to get in action. The perfect sleep happens when we get up fresh. So those who prefer sleeping late and getting up early, please give yourselves 6–7 hours of sleep to ensure your body and soul are on the right track to achieve your purpose in (this) life. Those who refuse to wake up even after a rested sleep, get moving, otherwise you may never be able to run and reach your supreme destiny.

So all I am saying is that sleep is most important and

should be given enough attention.

We feel tired when we are not working at the optimised pace. This happens because the body is being underutilised and does not get the encouragement to push itself faster. We have to at some point ask what our body is saying. This will be covered in the next book called *My Body*.

Here I should tell you that our bodies need attention so that we can fulfil our soul's path.

Our soul needs our body to ensure that the path is walked on and we ultimately understand what it takes for us to be one – Body and Soul, for the final goal to be fulfilled. That is, to be reunited with the source. The source eagerly awaits the souls, which left it many centuries ago, so that it also grows from the experiences it wanted to learn from.

The journey back seems very complicated for most of us but it is the most simple to carry out. All we need to do is follow our hearts' wishes and, in order to follow our heart, we need to have a sharp ear to understand/hear what the heart is saying without being clouded by any other million voices.

The ears are sharpened at the start of our journey back, so if you have experienced work happening on your 'ear' during meditation or during sleep, then you know that you are on your journey back. Your experiences are almost complete and only residues are left to be cleared up. We will all complete this journey. There is no race hence no question of who comes first or last. Completing the journey is the best reward one can get.

There can't be anything in this world that won't reach back to the source where it all started. Sooner or later we get back. The coming back ceremony is a celebration like no other. The welcome is so spectacular, so grand and so beautiful. The source's energy gets bigger and bigger as its own parts join back and become one.

So where do we go after that? Does this mean there is nothing after that? No, no; the beauty is that the ones in the source are eagerly waiting for their soul friends to return and will do everything possible to reach out and help them when they are lost and need direction to get back home. These are the 'Elders', the masters, the Gods as we know them; they will always be around to help and lend support when ever we need. It is not OK to feel that there is no one like me since each and every particle has come from the same source, the 'Source'. The source is a homogenous mixture and in the purest stage one cannot differentiate any parts of it. So how can you be any different form your enemy or your friend or father? We are all the same. Everything on this planet is the same if you see where I am coming from.

Now if we are the same, why do we feel and look so different? Why are there so many opposites like good and bad, beautiful and ugly, short and tall? The answer to this is that the opposites are the experiences we need to undergo, to understand what is meant by 'maintaining balance'. The balance in all of us is there in things that we are confident about. Anything else, we either overdo or under do.

Our life is so ridiculously simple to understand; yet we can't differentiate as to what is our free will and what was intended by us from the time before we decided to take birth. We will always be in a dilemma until we learn to listen to our hearts. Following your gut is closest to listening to your heart but when your head simultaneously works with your gut, you generally take a wrong decision.

★

The times have come when the old should be remembered and the new added to what was forgotten. Make a few amends here and there and you will have a world that is a better embodiment of its beauty and true nature. People have to understand the reasons for the things and situations that happen to them. First comes the realisation – that I am not just a being on earth, I am much more. Then comes the belief that you have much more power and much more work cut out for yourself than you had earlier thought belonged to others. You know by now that there are angels and the cycle of karma is all around you. Your karmic cycle gets shorter and shorter and you are able to make out the cause and effect in a matter of days rather than waiting for entire lifetimes.

You then move ahead on the path that you think/know will take you to your mission. Most men want to enlighten all others around them. While others want to seclude themselves from the rest to enjoy the vast and beautiful experiences on their own. Which category do you fall into? Don't say none, because at one point of your life or another you will realise, that you do fall under one of them. Your chances are guaranteed because you are reading this book. You have already read other similar books and thus you will be directed one day to the destiny that awaits you.

> 'We can only see the end of the road when we are near it. We can see the beginning until we are too far from it; so we see only what we can.'

## WE ARE ALL IN IT TOGETHER

*Message given by William*

We believe what we do is based on our background and social circle that we belong to. Well, how we do a certain task is primarily what those components determine. 'What' is still governed by what an individual needs to accomplish in this lifetime. A king and a beggar may need to do one common thing in their life, for example; both need to understand the need to give and share, to understand the value of being content with what they already have.

However, how they go about fulfilling that learning is far from being similar. The beggar is poor, lives a hard life, and has no shame or ego to ask for help from others. While the king has the most comfortable life, has much ego, and has many people looking up to him as a role model to follow. The learning the beggar needs to accomplish will be through the days when he has little food and also has to feed his companion or friend who is equally hungry. He needs to bow down in front of people he is envious of and ask them for food, clothing or money. His way of learning 'being content' is by realizing that even in his current state he has a lot to be thankful about.

For the king on the other hand, he needs to learn to give/ share his riches with the people he rules. He needs to learn the art of being content with what he has rather than focussing on gaining more control, power and money than what he already has. He needs to accept that other kings whom he may despise can be treated with respect and he can gain a lot by attaining their friendship.

The essence of this message is to know and think about what we need to do or learn rather than being stuck with the thought and restrictions of 'how'. We will understand what we need to do in other chapters of this book; for now just think about how many people are trying to do what you are also doing. Just notice the difference in this 'how' part.

*Message given by Archangel Michael*

We are all here; yes we are all here together. For you and for the sake of ensuring the path of learning is brought out in the open with splendour and beauty. The path becomes so clear and reachable that many lost ones are able to see it from a distance. The ease with which we sip a cup of coffee or tea and know how hot the liquid is, has becomes second nature to us and so we take it in our stride easily. The path of living and doing what becomes the destiny of our existence on the earth plane is so safe and fool proof that even if we forget a turn at any junction the next many junctions will remind us of the missed turn. The time we take to understand what we missed makes us value how important each step of the path is. When we go down that route we soak in all that is necessary and this learning, in turn, becomes second nature to us. The more we tell or remind ourselves of the bigger pattern in our life the more missed routes we would walk on and experience. This is the process of reminding ourselves what we have been experiencing in this life that has bothered us and has been reoccurring in our life. The pattern becomes easy if we think in isolation and meditate to find that pattern. One can opt for guidance from others but remember they will only ask you what you tell them about, nothing more. The half-truth would lead to half-baked solutions; however it's OK to try them out even when we know that at least 50 per cent of the journey can be achieved. The remaining 50 per cent would then need to be walked on by you and will need continuous motivation of self so that the remaining journey is completed. We do not need to run and we do not need to come first. All we need to do is be happy that we are walking on a map laid by us many years ago. We are making it possible to reach the destination or home of the existence of all that there is. The destination or 'source' is waiting for its particle to be reunited. The way that I see it is that you, yes, 'you' are going about experiencing what you wanted to experience and you are now understanding the importance of each and every turn. Now that you know what you need to do, it is important for you to remind yourself that what we do today will help you reach back to the source.

## CAN WE UNLEARN?

*Message given by William*

After we have achieved what our purpose of life is, can we again fall back and unlearn or complicate our previous learning? The answer to that question is 'No'. Once we have learnt that everyone has a purpose and learning, we stop looking outside for our problems. We look inwards to find the root cause of the issue so that we can fix it ourselves and deal with the outside situation. We will never be able to blame others for our misery. Now, if we see inwards and outwards to the people surrounding us, how many would have learnt this lesson; one or two, maximum! Well, those people are the examples we have chosen to remind ourselves of what we need to learn. The rest of the people have to learn other important lessons before they graduate and come to a level to understand this particular lesson.

Coming back to my opening question; *can we unlearn*? No, we can't. We keep adding layers to our understanding. However, the truth and learning in its most fine/smallest form would still hold its meaning and purpose for our existence and evolution.

After we learn the lesson we had chosen for ourselves, we either die or we seek more (lessons). The ones who seek more are required to take some rest. They may seem lazy or unbothered for sometime/years before they start their journey again. We are going to see such people and we would be such people; hence it is important for us to realise the importance of acting upon what we came here to learn and at the same time provide rest to our body and soul to move forward to the next level of our learning.

Eventually we may give up our bodies to reach back to the source and fill up all our lessons and experiences back into the big jar of experiences of the civilisations that came before us. The more we have to give back to the source the better. Even if we are able to learn one important lesson then we have contributed to the reason why this world exists!

# 13

# You

*Message given by Soloris*

The understanding of how a person can be in many roles is the true understanding of a person. Give him all the roles to play and you will see different sides of him. Yet if he plays just one role at all times he becomes sluggish, irritating, boring, monotonous and not to mention – a perfectionist (as per him at least).

Don't fall into the trap of allowing just one role to be played by you in this life. Take on as many roles or situations to discover yourself. After all, if you don't know yourself completely then how are you to trust yourself completely? If you don't understand your fears than how are you going to overcome them? If you don't know what you like then how on earth will you ever find the love of your life that you have been looking for?

## HOW TO START YOUR JOURNEY INWARDS

*Message given by William*

The places are many but the names are few. The people are many but we know just a few. Why not everybody? Why not all of us, why not all the places? Why not all the countries we know? Well, for one simple reason – that we don't want to know all. We choose a few, some choose many while some very little. Then some may choose not to know anyone at all. They are just happy knowing themselves. Happiness lies in what you are happy with, not what others think that you should be happy with or how you should be happy.

Why do we need a marriage, a child or a job in our lives? Why is it a must for us to go on in our lives? And once married why do we want other men/women in our lives? Why aren't we just happy with the one we are married to? Or rather why is it wrong to think of other men/women post marriage? Why so many rules? Who imposed them? You? Me? No? Well, think about it!

Yes, it is you and me. Be open about how you feel. Be brave enough to let your feelings rule your life if that is what makes you happy. Yet sometimes we sacrifice our own happiness for the sake of guilt for others. We don't want to take risks for the sake of our marriage, our children, our jobs, our lives. So we sit it out. We wait for the end to arrive with nothing to look forward to and no happiness to be looked for. We become mechanical. We become like robots. Doing what is necessary for us to do. Just doing our jobs – that is to live and to live for the sake of others. But till when? Till your own breaking point?

*Message given by Archangel Michael*

Please don't tell yourself that we are at the mercy of circumstances. Please don't allow yourself to believe that you can't control everything that happens in your life. Because you have the power and you have the energy to control each and everything that happens to you. Where on earth can you find a place or person who can control your life more than you? Where in heaven can you find a source that can walk the path you walk? Where will you see the consequences of your actions? All the questions lead you to one common place, 'your conscience', 'your body', 'your soul', 'your aura', and 'your surroundings'.

All and everything in you and around you are the best people and places that control and formulate our strategy to live our life as intended when we had no limitations; when we saw everything so clearly that each consequence could be thought of and planned. If there was any doubt, it could be answered by the Gods and if there was anything that was not correct then it was corrected before we took this life. You, my dear friend, have been blessed to be with yourself and the surrounding that you have chosen for yourself when you were in the best position to decide what's best for you. Acknowledge this fact and reach out to yourself. There is nothing to be afraid of and there is nothing to run away from.

*Message given by Soloris*

People try to seek their answers everywhere else apart from within themselves. Deep down they know that the answers lie within them yet they choose to ignore themselves because looking out is much easier and less scary than peeking in. Don't run away from yourselves. Let yourself be understood by your own self. No one else will matter then. You will not depend on others but you will know that you have yourself to depend on. Now you will feel more confident and much stronger than you have ever felt.

*Message given by William*

If we could see our own futures, how wonderful would it be to look at how we would fare if we played by the rules of others. How would you like to see yourself ten years down the line – looking older, wiser, beaten up, as though the world rested on your shoulders, and yet you don't give a damn about anything or anyone although you have to because this is what you are used to now. You – yourself – stand completely forgotten.

The world is moulded in a selfish pattern and so are the people who designed the moulds. They – the people or others – don't want you to think about yourself and what makes you happy. So man has eventually forgotten that he himself only exists because he exists for others. The latest fashion, the trendy make-up, the fashionable shoes, the over expensive dinners, the gadgets, the cars, the over indulgent parents, the sprawling houses – all entail attention away from yourself. And this is taking the limelight away from the poor mere 'U' in you.

Now this does not mean that you do what makes you most happy, like sitting and watching TV in your shorts on your holiday and not taking a bath. No sir! This is exactly opposite to what I mean. And I want you to understand how you can make yourself 'happy' by spending quality time with yourself and yourself alone. Do something that you have been wanting to do but have been putting away for too long. Go to the gym, go for that walk in nature, go for that swim or just sit all by yourself without doing anything – like reading the paper or a book or looking at other people around you or just doodling on a piece of paper. Just be quiet for a while and relax and sit all by yourself doing nothing. While you are sitting, feel as though there is no time and space. Just feel yourself from within. Find your pulse and be with your heart. You don't have to think anything. Just be. Close your eyes and feel your inner body, your inner strength. I am sure most of you would freak out after the first fifteen minutes, but just do it. Since you want to be truthful to yourself, you will realise that you have never really spent this much time, paying attention and giving importance to 'you'.

Try it. There is no harm in trying to be with yourself. You will love it, I promise you. Do it everyday. Day after day and feel the change with which you look at yourself daily. And also how your body responds to your daily love. Good luck because here and from now on your inner journey starts. And the best part is that, for this kind of journey, you don't even need a backpack.

## KNOW THY SELF

*Message given by William*

Take your self liberally and you will find all the peace there is to find. Take yourself seriously and you will miss out a whole lot of fun there is by you to be experienced. You are the role model for yourself. You are what you have made yourself into.

I want you to do a task for me today:

Throughout the day (for one day) I want you to think of words that describe you. Make your own bio-data – the kind you have never made. Make it so that anyone reading would know the person, the human being you really are.

Write down everything – big or small, bad or good, beautiful or ugly, sad or happy. Just write yourself on a piece of paper, listen to your inner self; in fact, write to your inner self and have a dialogue with yourself. Find out who you really are – without the degrees and diplomas, without any religious ties, without your father and mother, without your spouse and kids, without your job and money, without your car and your house – just you, plain simple you.

## WHO ARE YOU?

It is very necessary that you have completely understood the above task so reread it if you want to. Just consciously think about yourself throughout the day. You don't need to do this every minute or every second, but just be aware of the task you need to finish in one day's time and jot down whatever comes to your mind, whenever it comes to your mind.

Do not imagine what you could be or what you will be. Just deal with what you are at the present. This may sound easy but you will come to know, really know, for the first time – the kind of a being you are. Be truthful because it is after all going to be just between the two of you – that is you and you yourself!

Start with sentences that begin with 'I am _____'. Do not use sentences that begin with either of these – I hate, I love, I should, I will, I can.

Just, I am....

The next set of instructions I shall urge you to read will be after the (above) task is completed.

Take this day to rethink and recompile the list you have made. Edit it for yourself if you feel the need to; just make sure that you are not feeling bad/guilty for writing something that you are not sure of or that is not true. Just do this today and make your list about yourself foolproof. You can do it is by simply running down your finger through all that you have written and by saying out loud what you have written one by one. If your heart does not object and feels that you have written the truth you can move on to the next item you have written. Cross check your list with your heart before you move on to the next phase.

Now pin this up on the inside of your cupboard and remind yourself of who you really are by looking at this list every morning before you head for work or before you start your day. It's a place you cannot miss because you'll need your clothes everyday and everyday you will find yourself looking at who you really are.

You would also need to segregate the good and the bad. Keep the good ones on the left and the bad ones on the right. Against each bad thing – write down the opposite of it to realise that you have already made a change from the bad towards the good by first putting it in black and white. There is no need to hurry but you do need to take things off this list (the bad ones) one by one. The left side should start to increase slowly and gradually.

Convert yourself; convert your habits that you dislike about yourself slowly with focus and concentration. You can only do it when you are conscious of the fact that you are doing something that you dislike in yourself. You need to be able to catch yourself in the act of thinking/doing what it is you feel is bad about you. Once you do this, restrain from this thought/action and then start to avoid it fully and completely.

Love yourself and be true to yourself and not for anybody else. You know everything – what is right and what is not – just follow your footsteps. You don't need anybody else to show you the direction you need to take.

Why be unhappy unnecessarily when you know you can be happy always? Why jump to conclusions when there are other ways to conclude? You are yourself stopping your own growth – be it mentally, physically, emotionally or spiritually. You are the driving force for yourself. Nobody else can drive you. Nobody can take control of the steering wheel of your life and steer you in no direction at all. It is you who needs to get up and get ready to make the changes your life is screaming out for. You know all your problems and within your heart are all the answers.

## DON'T UNDERESTIMATE THE GOOD IN YOU

*Message given by Archangel Gabriel*

The world has witnessed numerous changes. It is because of

the words that have been in use and because of the light that is spreading from each one of you. A light of pure joy and pure love. You have yourselves to blame for things that go wrong but why do you not take credit for the many things that go right? Don't be shy or feel as though you are gloating. In this heightened state of consciousness you will soon realise how good it feels to own up to all the good that you have done.

Why we fish for compliments from others is because we are trained to believe that self-praise is no praise at all. That is the reason why we look for appreciation outside of us. Do good and say that you do good. You can be humble about it but you can't go wrong with it. You just need to know not to overdo it or exaggerate. This is easy to understand because once you start taking credit for what you do, you will not feel the need to exaggerate.

On the other hand, you would work harder and better to achieve your own level of competence that you have set up for yourself. It is not good to keep quiet about all the good or nice things we do. We need our own words to appreciate our actions. To appreciate ones own self is simply and completely divine. So don't hold yourself back when asked what all good you have done. Remember that you are a part of the source and you have been made perfectly in the most divine sense. You cannot go wrong about sharing how good you are – after all we all compliment God, don't we? We need to be doing the same for ourselves.

Find your heart, listen to your heart and you will stop

being bothered by your problems. They may still exist but they won't be of any impact on you as you will simply move on. Now the question arises – how do I listen to my heart? Well, if you remember, we have already covered that in a previous chapter. The one where you can say 'yes' or 'no' to understand how your heart responds to a lie and how it responds to the truth.

## THE BEGINNING OF A MASTER

*As narrated by William, a Soul Guide*

My journey as a soul started with the first light of the sunshine. I was brown in colour and was a beautiful sea stone. I was able to completely polish and smoothen myself with the waves riding on me every day. But then I saw an even prettier stone that was blue in colour. To my amazement it was not even close to being smooth in texture. I thought to myself, why can I not be as pretty as that blue stone instead of being as polished as I am now? The answer did not come to me at that point of time.

I waited years and years until I was completely submerged in the waters and dissolved fully with the sands around me. That is when I died – as a rock. It took me almost a thousand years to die as a rock. When I reached above and viewed my life as that brown smooth rock, I then understood the meaning and significance of the rough blue pretty rock.

I was in love with the blue rock because it had everything that I didn't have – good and bad. I did not appreciate the good in me but only wanted to trade for what was good in that blue stone. I, however, realised that being good or bad doesn't really make a difference. It is the oneness of you with your thoughts that makes the difference.

# 14

# We Are All One

*Don't believe me? Read on to see my perspective....*

One begins to wonder why we eat, breathe and sleep everyday. Everyday!! Why do we need to follow certain things like cleaning our teeth, our bodies or our minds everyday? Have you ever wondered? Think before you answer.

Read below so as to understand the point I'll make.

The light within the cosmos has given us so much strength that we can endure much pain without crying out and yet so little wisdom, that we keep crying out. Is that the way you feel about yourself or anyone else around you? You are not mistaken. The world largely consists of two categories of people – the ones who read and the ones who don't.

There are a lot of similarities between the two but the differences are what are most interesting.

Let's look at the similarities now. The ones who read do not like the ones who do not read and vice versa. This is because they feel that they are above them. The reading group feels that the other group cannot and will never be able to understand the larger concepts of life and will not be imaginative enough to imagine what worlds are written about in books. The non-reading group however feels that they are far superior than the other group because they don't need to read from others' experiences what they can themselves experience. They feel that they don't need a 'guide' in their lives and they tend to be more adventurous and outgoing.

The best part is that the difference lies not in the thinking but in the way they lead their lives. You will find the first group filling their entire day with weird thoughts and consequences that may never occur in their lives. On the other hand, the second group starts their days by simply putting one foot forward and not over thinking about the situations they may have to face. They are more light-hearted and jolly throughout the day. They will love the surprises the day has to offer and thus will fulfil their every desire in the best possible manner they seem fit.

The first group will try to fit in and then realise from the experiences of others (i.e. from books) how and why they are not able to handle their day differently. They will choose to colour what is meant to be coloured whereas the second group will colour all that can be coloured!

So why the hell am I going on about the people who don't read in such a positive fashion?! Well, for one so that the people who do read (and that my friend is *you*) can read this and realise that your group is not superior to theirs. Someone needs to bridge the gap so that since we can read, we may as well understand the need for all to be one and not think lowly of the ones who don't read. Secondly, have you ever heard of such an argument before? No? So, there! That is my second reason!

Now why has this all come up in this book? So we can all journey towards finding one path for all of us and for being able to walk the path with the rest of us. The everyday routine that we talked about in the beginning is only one more example of walking together on the same path. All following the same routine but in different countries, in different manners and in different time zones. Yet all follow it, no matter where. That is the whole lesson, the crux of this book, the crux of you and me.

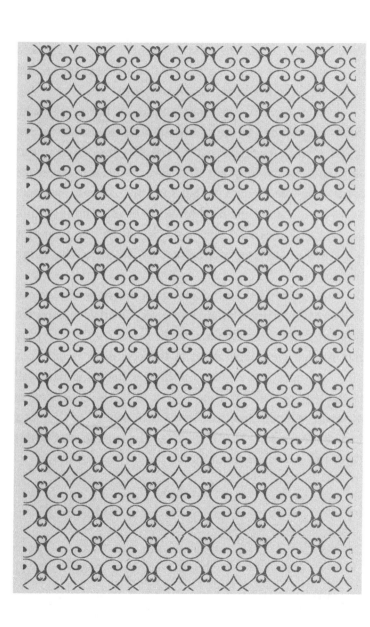

# 15

# The Masters and You

*Message given by William*

The people who come to walk on this earth plane to spread wisdom and truth of the game of life are the masters who had to deal with a lot of issues before they did what was necessary for them to reach out to millions of people. For example, Jesus Christ had a humble beginning, far from any correct wisdom and the teachings of true knowledge. He had to travel far and wide to remind himself of what all he knew. Each step he took was disliked by the rulers of the time as they did everything in their control to stop him on his path.

His coming back was a reassurance to the people that his teachings were true and for people to have a lasting memory of the 'way' he showed to fellow mankind. Jesus was not perfect; he was not someone who was limitless or created out of magical powers of God. He was like all of us who came very close to understanding all that there is to know about how this worlds ticks. What is necessary to do and what is not. Letting go of any limiting thoughts and beliefs to do all that one feels is impossible to be done by an ordinary man. He was a great soul and now is one with the source. He may come back to the earth plane but not for another 100 centuries. OK, let us see how could he share a small portion of food with hundreds of people. He could because he believed he could, without a single thought passing his mind that it was not possible. That is how the universe around us functions. Every object and being is created for us so we can use them in a number of ways to carry out what we truly want to do. Seek their help – ask food to be tasty, ask your friend to help you, seek the help of the pen to help you write with a clear handwriting. All will become the truth if you believed; they would work for you as intended without any interference of anything to come in the way of you achieving your destiny.

*Message given by Archangel Michael*

If God could come on the earth plane then couldn't He just come and resurrect everything at once? Don't you think it would be possible for God to do that? The answer to that is 'Gods wouldn't enter the game of life'. They need not be a part of it to ensure they are able to run it smoothly and evolve themselves and the life game, in a manner that all of us reach to the finish or the end state. What goes in comes out; for the source it's the opposite – what goes out comes in. It takes centuries for that to happen but it does. That is the will of God and that is the true game of life.

So who were 'Jesus' or 'Buddha' or 'Sai Baba' if they were not Gods? They did everything right, became examples for millions and gave help to the people who asked for their help. The great powers they possessed to heal and to give, does give them a greater appeal than normal humans. I don't disagree. They were messengers from God. Their purpose was aligned not to their learning alone but also to align the purpose of many on the earth plane to resurrect a situation gone out of hand after reaching earth.

All the great masters who have taken birth also had to deal with pain and suffering. They had to face challenges in their path to fulfil their purpose. The learning, which they had to fully accept and practice, is evident in the life they led. Now who is denying them any lesser importance than Gods for the fellow mankind? Since they were instrumental in making many people get back to the right path. However they were not 'Gods'. They lived in the limitations of the physical body. They had to learn the true purpose of their life and had to fight it out to fulfil their destiny and they succeeded.

## *Message given by Soloris*

If all people believed in one thing to be right, then all the situations of learning would have been the same. Experience and learning would not have evolved as much as when you consider the other extremity of the situation. The balance can be achieved in two ways – the shortcut is to follow what others say. Or experience one side, fully experiment the possibilities of that situation and then by going to the other extremity and fully exploring that situation in a similar manner as the first. What you will end up with would be the best of both the worlds and will live that situation in complete and wholesome balance.

The balance in life can be achieved in both ways described above. Not all aspects need to be experienced by one particle of the source (the soul). What this means is that not all experiences that each one has to do/achieve will need an experience of polarities. There is so much to do and experience, we learn from each other as well. The true learning each particle needs to get will be acquired by the second path. For the remaining, we can learn from others.

Each one of us is a master of situations and experiences. The ones we master, we help others learn. For the ones we don't need to master, we learn from others. There would be many instances where learning from others may not give us enough confidence and wisdom to cross the landmarks necessary for our evolution. In which case we move to the second method to achieve the right balance.

Unless all in a soul group reach the peak potential or the number of ticks are completed in the checklist created for the group, this learning continues. The source will be the destiny but only if we are able to learn the path of truth and act as if we came here to rule. We cannot outgrow or outlive experiences, as there is no way we can be more than the source.

Why are there only a few masters or gurus that walk on the planet preaching and showing how to live and treat well?

As we have teachers so we have masters/guides/gurus. As we have the people of the world at large so we have students. I shall explain with the example of teachers and students. Teachers are always less and students more in any school. The same applies to the masters and the general public. Some want to learn so they follow a particular master/guide. Some want to remain illiterate or are not aware of these masters or guides and so they do not approach them. Even in today's world there are many people/children who are not allowed to or who do not wish to or who can't study. Not all the people can be approached by the teachers. So the ratio between the number of masters or guides to the number of people on this earth is just like the ratio of students and teachers in the school. Don't feel that a guide will contact you just as you know that a teacher wouldn't contact you. You need to show the effort and you will be helped in all the ways you want help.

Why do you think there is no one you can look up to and ask all questions from?

This question is also related to the previous answer. If you have anyone that you trust and who you know will give you help that you want, you need to ask for it. Guides and masters are all around you. You just need to know that they are. Each one of us is surrounded by beautiful angels. Know that they love you and will make things happen for you if you only let them. Wait for their signals, look and be aware of their messages. You have it all – the power to receive and to give. Utilise it. The entire universe is for you. Do you think that the cosmos is so greedy that it will not give you what you desire? The world that you live in is very powerful; thus it makes you very powerful – ask and you shall receive. Ask from the universe, ask from nature, ask from yourself and you will never be disappointed.

## THE MASTER IN YOU

*Message given by Archangel Michael*

We are now enjoying the fruits of the seeds we once sowed many generations ago. I am saying this without a single iota of sarcasm. We are better emotionally, mentally and physically. We can conquer all feats and we can win all battles as we are equipped and have been trained to do so. We are the soldiers who know what it takes to defend our land. Worthy of winning all the battles, we are emotionally charged to shoo away all negative thoughts. You – 'yes, *you*' – can go out and tell the world that there is love all around you. You have the power to undo all that has gone wrong. You are capable of saying – 'I have arrived', at the peak of your voice and feel it.

But why didn't it all seem cosy up till now? There are a few alterations necessary to make the most well-fitted outfit. So your alterations were the small upheavals you have experienced to reach the stage you are in now. I have to say, we are alive and a life is what we will live each passing moment. I have only myself to bring a smile on my face. I have me for making myself believe that I can climb that big mountain. I am the best piece of God's creation and I am here to bring out the best pieces in others. I am Here!

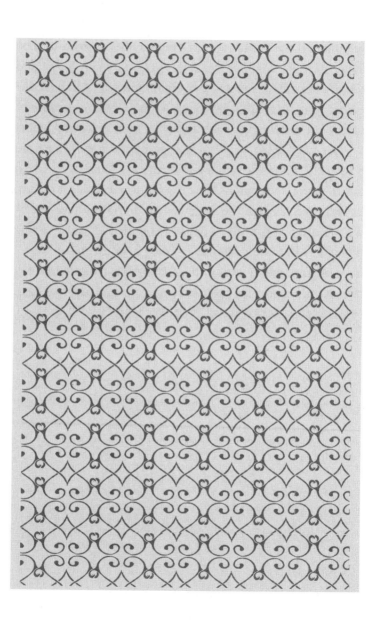

# 16

# Don't Wait. Act Now: Message from Tom, the Free Spirit

There are times when you know that there is nobody around you who really knows you or with whom you can talk about yourself or your feelings. I have felt it many times and every time I have felt this, it hurt my heart and I felt as though my heart had suddenly shrunk in size. It felt as though there was a heavy weight instead of a beating heart. I felt as though the whole world was of no use because 'I' was not part of it. At such times, I wished that I were not there anymore. I had wished so many times that I had never taken birth and had not chosen life over anything other that was on offer. But then, as I passed on into a different world altogether I realised what a stupid fool I had been throughout the years that I had been given on earth.

I could not understand the one simple thing that while living, you are always supposed to be alone. No matter what, no matter when, another being cannot help you in what you are and what you do to yourself. It is only after looking at my previous life from a different or higher perspective, that I now realise how I wasted my time finding the right person or the right moment to talk about what I wanted to say about what I felt. I kept waiting for an opportunity to arise and kept waiting without trying to talk to those who already were around me. It was my mistake, my fault; I should not have waited. In fact there was no need to even think that I needed to wait.

All I ever needed was always all around me but I never saw anything. Instead of pushing through the leaves to look at the sky above I just kept waiting for a breeze to push apart the leaves so I could see the sky above. I did nothing, nothing on my own. No effort. No will. No motivation. No encouragement to myself from myself. Just a really long wait for something to happen to me... anything to happen to me. Only when I died, did I realise how stupid I had been. How blind I had been. Now I am coming back to earth to learn what I did not learn in the last lifetime and that is to make efforts and to go for it, whatever it be.

So, if you know anyone who has done everything well in their lives but they still don't have what they deserve – well you will know that it could be someone who is just bent to make things wait for him instead of him waiting for them. He may work hard and may do everything he or she possibly can and should but the things he wants will wait for him as he had made himself wait for them in his previous life. I am ready to take the world by its horns and just do whatever it is to make this waiting game go away. After my lesson is learnt I will get everything I want, when I want it. After I work for it. That is my goal. So stop waiting for things, otherwise no matter how much you wait for them, things are going to make you wait.

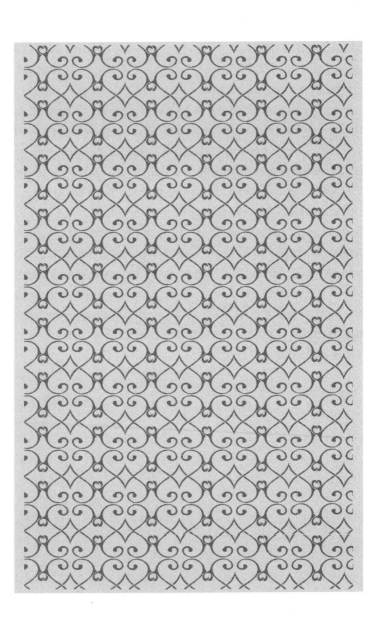

# 17

# Message from GOD

How lovingly I have made you and how indifferently you treat yourselves. I made you with pride and with purpose and it is no excuse that you have forgotten because you have not. You are reminded about yourselves each and every day yet you fail to recognise the voice of God. My voice. I don't know why you do this because you are always in your own hands.

Each person living or not, each article living or destroyed, has been my conception. I have made all of you perfect for all that is around you and made you just the way you should be. Not a single flaw do I see in my making. So why do you see so many flaws in yourself? You are all good. Each one of you. You are all perfect. Had you not been perfect, would you call me God? Answer me in your thoughts and I shall reply back. You are how you should have been. You are not to change for the sake of others but only for yourself and only if you know it is helping you in the upliftment of your soul. You are not here just to be and to play the part of a human. You are here because you have played the part of a human being way too many times and have come to realise that there is more to yourself that you need to excel at. That you are more than a person who cannot do everything and also finds things impossible to do. You have made a wonderful, long, adventurous journey to be where you are right now. You should be proud of your achievements but also know that there is a long yet different way to go now. So what is it that you are afraid of? Change? Yes, change is the answer. No one likes to change the way they are. But you know what? I made you perfect when you were born. But once you are born it is your duty, your responsibility, to make yourself perfect in the world that you live in. Whatever you do or don't do, make yourself perfect at it. Whatever you think or don't think, make your thinking perfect. What you are afraid of most (change) will happen to you again and again till you learn to change yourself, till you learn that change is the only way of life.

So what if your habits are very good; there are still thoughts in you that are not so good. Go out. Explore the minds and thoughts of other people. Take them in, listen to them, explore them, discover how wrong you have been and be open to change the part that is wrong in you.

## OH MY GOD! (OMG)

'Oh My God', we say. But do we really mean it when we say it? What if we really were to meet God one day and he asks us why do we keep saying 'Oh My God' whenever something very bad or very nice happens? What would you answer? I would personally say that I say it because it just automatically comes out of me without realisation and without any thought.

Well if you are really saying it, are you meaning it as well? That God is yours?

My God! Never thought of it that way, did you?!

Well, YES, to answer you from my perspective or God's perspective. I am YOUR God. But please don't *just* say it. I want you to feel me too. I will feel nice if you were to say it while actually meaning what you are saying. Please, would you do this one favour for me and make me feel nice every time you were to say 'Oh My God'?

For once, I will tell you a story, the story of a shoemaker and a joker.

The shoemaker was a very wise man and did not get in the way of other people's business. The joker on the other hand was also good at his job but always got in the way of others whether they wanted him to or not. This he failed to recognise. So on he went with his life trying to make people laugh and at the same time getting in their way as much as he could. One day a wise king called the chief shoemaker and asked him to make a beautiful pair of golden shoes for him. The shoemaker sought the help of the best shoemakers and gave them each a task that needed to be done. Now, our shoemaker was amongst the team of the shoemakers and he set forth to do his job calmly and diligently.

The next morning when the shoes had to be tried for fitting for the king, they all dressed up in fine clothes and reached the gates of the king's palace. To their dismay they had to halt because of the joker who was standing in their way. The joker unknowingly delayed the shoemakers by telling them his jokes and showing them tricks they were not interested in seeing. On they went as soon as the joker finished but they had already become late for their appointment with the king.

The chief shoemaker saw this as an opportunity to make the others understand that it was he who would go to the king and that they did not need to accompany him. At the next available appointment he met up with the king who asked him why he hadn't brought the shoes earlier. He replied, 'I have many servants who work for me, yet not one is fit enough to look me in the eye and say that what I do is wrong. How can I, a mere servant of yours, show you a bunch of people who are as ignorant as I? But I come with the will of God to serve you and only you. And that is why I have been blessed to have this opportunity to be with you and present to you the shoes that will bring honour to me and my life.'

Not satisfied with the answer, the king asked for the other helpers to be present and asked them why they had not made it to the appointment earlier. Our shoemaker replied, 'Dear King, it is a great honour to be present in the same room as you and as your humble servant, I would like to say that it was your gate that delayed us in our appointment that day. At your palace gates was a joker who was beautiful in every manner you can expect a joker to be, but he did not have the sense of timing and delayed us unknowingly. It wasn't his fault according to him and it wasn't our fault in our opinion. It was just the perfection of the state that was brought from no fault of anyone that you got to meet us all and we could meet you and share a snippet of our lives. This dialogue of us talking and you listening is the perfect outcome of the faults that nobody made.'

So, why do we always have to see whose fault it is and who to blame? Look at the situation it has brought you to and know that it's the perfect situation that you have helped create due to no fault of yours or of others.

The objectives of the life's understandings are not to forgive others but to find and forgive one's own self. Only when we know that we are at fault, in any and every manner, do we tend to forgive others. So to forgive oneself is the highest sense of achievement. The wrongs in others make the rights in us.

This is exactly what you had decided to get into, this

messy affair, this painful relationship, this idiotic self, these pitiful situations have all been created by you.

So if you are in pain, you need to get out of it. So if you are in a messed up affair, you need to un-clutter it. So if you are in a pitiful situation, you need to come out of it stronger and with more confidence. So if you are so idiotic and make the same mistakes again and again, you need to begin to learn from them.

Whatever it is that you are finding difficult, you need to just pen it down. Use different words or adjectives for what you are feeling towards the issue. Just one word and not full sentences. Write them all down. Then start eliminating similar meaning words and ultimately you will have the entire situation that will boil down to just one word. If you have more than one word you can pick the word that holds more relevance/importance to you. Circle it and darken the circle and think about this word for a long time.

*For example:*

If health is your main issue, you could write words such as:

- Difficult (to maintain the body)
- Consistency (to be consistent in the diet or exercising)
- Limits (of how much to eat, what to eat, how much to exercise)

Now since consistency and limits are the factors that contribute in making it difficult to maintain the body, we can cross out these two and concentrate on the word 'difficult'.

Once you are able to picture this word in your mind, think what is the one word solution for this word or even the opposite of the word. Yes! That is the purpose of this situation that you are currently in. You have created this situation especially for yourself. This is one more chapter that you as a soul, need to learn. You have planned it all right, even before taking birth on this planet.

You cannot be a melody that can't be sung unless it is sung.
You can't be that flower that blooms unless you are the bloom.
You can't be the rain unless you are wet.
You can't be on the move unless you are still.
You can't be on the moon unless you are on the earth.
You can't be in love unless you are love!

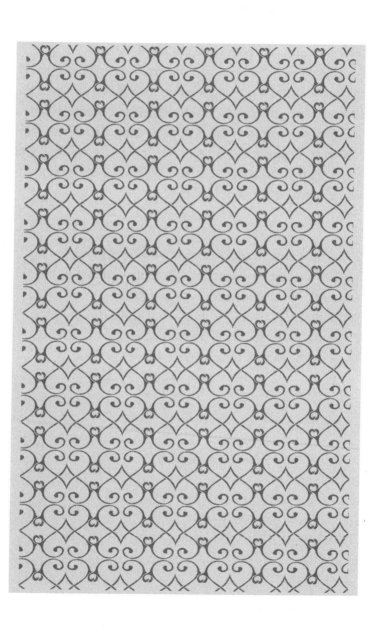

# 18

# No 'One' Is God

*Message given by Soloris*

Why have we not been to work all day long? What is it that keeps us going, all day long? How does our clock go tick-tock? How do we go on living a life when there is no intent of living the life we want to live? How do we perform well even when we know we haven't really worked hard for it? How do we come to terms with our problems, dilemmas and our own selves' everyday? Why is life so tough for some and so easy for some? Why don't I meet the girl or boy I always dreamed of?

How come I only get ahead after I have slogged and slogged and yet others get there so easily? Why am I so gullible and why are others so strong-willed? Why do I have to look out for others when I myself am not comfortable and safe? Why do I have to confront the world everyday as though it is my enemy? Why can't the sun always shine on me?

Why does God not listen to what I have to say? Why do we even believe in God if he doesn't listen? Who do we talk to if there is no God? Who will help me if there is no God? Is there really a God or is this all there is to life – nothing more to look at, just living this one life – be it in misery or in pain. Just this one chance at life. If I do have just one life then why isn't it good and beautiful and happy? Why so much pain, why so much heartache, why no love, why no smiles, why the ill health? Why, why, why, why always me?

Why only me? What have I done? How do I undo it? Why, why, why? Who can help me? Anyone? No is the answer to all the questions asked. No, No, No, there is no God. Well there is no *one* God. Because God is divided equally between you and me and between all those who walk this earth. So yes. He will listen to you, only if you know who you are telling your problems to. If you call a wrong number and ask for God then you will never really get to speak to him. But, if you were to speak to God as if he were you, a part of you, inside you, you will begin to realise that not only does he listen to you but he also answers you. You will hear a faint tiny voice that will tell you what you should be doing. You need to be able to catch all the messages that manifest around you so that you know what your next step should be.

The God in you makes you manifest all that is around you. Ask for help and look around and see the different ways that you are helped. You just need to open your eyes to see what is being unfolded before you – anything, like birds chirping, like a smiling child, an advertisement on TV, a song on the radio, a conversation overheard, a joke, a message sent to your phone, a tree falling, a leaf floating, a stranger helping you, anything, anything at all.

You just need to be aware of the fact that there are messages all around you that will lead you on and make you happier. You just need to be aware. The knowledge alone that there are messages for you, around you, gives you the power to believe in the God within you who can manifest all this for you. Just for you. You of all the people know this secret now; use it for your own good and spread it to all those whose good you wish to see.

And don't ever worry if you are unable to catch a message. You will be given many opportunities, many chances to see these messages in your life. In fact, you will keep on getting these messages till you notice them. This is definitely not your only life on earth. Why would it be? What would be your purpose? Just to live and then die? What for? Who for? Why then the pain and suffering? Why then the hatred and jealousy? What for? Who for? No, No, No. You have a bigger purpose. A bigger plan! You have not been given birth to just die and be forgotten amongst the millions who die everyday.

★

If there comes a time when people no longer fear the unknown, then they will know that death is accomplishing a task or a learning. Then people would know what they needed to do to get whatever they wish for. If everything happens with their truest intent, then wouldn't this be the best place to live? It certainly wouldn't!

The reason is simple; no one would be happy or sad. No one would try to do things differently. No one would care about what will happen if they didn't succeed and stumble across so many other things that are important for all of us to learn; to firmly say 'I rule my emotion'. I rule 'my own self', and I rule 'everything around me'. When you truly rule, you have the power to understand everything that goes in and around the things you rule.

Now please understand; the picture above seems to be the ultimate state. To be one with the source. To be with God and to be God. Earth is our workshop, we can't be Gods here. Our ultimate destination is graduating from all workshops and being one with the source. So please accept your faults as they make us worthy of living on this earth plane. We cannot be Gods here. We can only pass on what we have learned in the manner we understand the truth. Always remember, the truth, as we know it, can have different flavours and dimensions. Please give yourself a pat on the shoulder when you see yourself taking in new forms of the truth. People who preach with limits and boundaries do a great job of imparting knowledge but lose out on their own growth. Only you decide what you need to learn. Follow your heart into a journey where everybody is equal. No one is God!

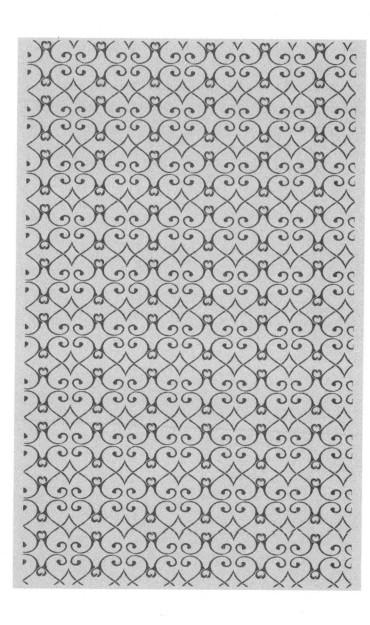

# 19

# The Secret of 2012

*Message given by William*

It was not a matter of the world coming to an end. It was how parts of 'you' were coming to a conclusion in the year 2012. As each of you sensed a shift in yourselves, the world too saw the shift in its being. So yes, that was the end everyone talked about but it was as twisted a truth as it possibly could be. Time and the nature of humans made this simple piece of information into something that was exaggerated and of no consequence. It was no surprise that people were actually waiting to see if the world came to an end or not.

We all look at everything from the outside, the exteriors, when we really should be looking at the most genuine and subtle interiors. That is where lies the truth – the untwisted, unexaggerated version.

The year 2012 would go down as the most important year for spirituality. It is the year that has begun the collective consciousness to be formed – consciously – among millions of people across the lands. It is the start, a beginning of a whole new era. Now for anything to start there has to be a finish to what was there prior to the start. So 2012 was both a marking of an end and a beginning of a new era.

*(The messages below were written in the year 2010, thus the difference in the tense. No changes have been made to these messages since they were first written.)*

Will there be enough experiences for God to say that I have experienced everything? Or is this just some other crap to explain that life goes on. Well the answer is – God doesn't know yet. He doesn't know whether the experiences he has felt through all of us are enough. He will take stock in December 2012, he will decide then. He will understand that experiences that he has are all that there is and will go back to the same grind if he feels he needs more of them, else every man on earth will experience God's powers in a manner that will be so beautiful and powerful that we will have a great time through the time.

If you think there is going to be calamity, destruction, floods and earthquakes or even World War III, then you are absolutely and completely wrong. The calamity or events, which one may perceive, would be internal, internal to your surroundings only and limited to you only. You and only you would understand the gravity of the situation. You and you alone would need to grow out of it. People, who think that a 'guide' will come to help them, need to understand that the guide is already in their hands. People who have not got access to this book will get the messages and answers through other sources.

It's all about knowing a new set of rules to play the game of life. What we believed would change. Our purpose and goals would change. Some good wise men will walk the earth and spread the message of the new rules to the world. This book will reach out to many millions and will play a huge part in spreading the knowledge needed in the world to undergo the transformation. I will not only be able to witness this but will also cherish the beauty of the change.

*Message given by Soloris*

Soloris says that the world as we know it would never come to an end because we have known the world in this form and nothing of this sort can come to an end unless we want it to end. People don't like changes in their lives yet they know that change is the only thing that remains constant. At the same time, people have the habit of not doing what they know they should be doing. They like to delay matters and do things in their own sweet fashion, waiting for a knock on the head that tells them the reason why they should be doing what they are avoiding to do. Most would ask – if the world is not coming to an end then what is so special about 2012? Well, the answer is simple. To see the change we need to be the change. So the extraordinary shift in ourselves to allow oneness and knowledge of 'us' to become one with ourselves will require a significant effort and change in our surroundings.

We will witness what we fear the most but the fear will go if we learn from it. For some the fear may be all engulfing; hence it's important to have an understanding of all aspects of 'your conscience' so that we learn to live with it and surpass the time the shift is taking place. Most of you will overcome your fears if you have managed to read so far. People who have not read this book will survive through many other means that others have created to tackle the upcoming milestone.

# 20

# A Message for Parents

*by Soloris*

How we saw ourselves as children usually comes to haunt us when we are adults. The same situations, the same environment, the same kind of people and the same thought process. What we need to do is to break the monotony. What we attract as children remains attached to us as adults as well. Now how can a child be told that? Well, the answer is simple. Once you have changed yourself as a parent and made conscious efforts to straighten up your life, according to the path of your life, you will begin to understand all that a child needs and requires. The kind of understanding you need to understand a kid's perspective is most important. You literally and sometimes very painfully need to be in their shoes and stay in their shoes so that you know what they want and the best way in which you can deliver it to them.

Bringing up a child is easy if you do it in an easy manner. The child should be aware of what to do and what not to do. He should be given the freedom to explore his body parts yet be told what is correct and how important it is for him to report back to you if anything or anyone infiltrates his privacy. At the same time, they should be told the positive sides of being in oneness with their bodies and the kind of love they should show towards their bodies. Make them realise what is good for the body and what is bad. This could be in terms of food, sexuality, religion, pains, punishments, etc.

Gradually they will begin to know what their body tries to tell them. They will be able to trust their bodies and vice versa. Their bodies will realise that they are being heard and thus feel well taken care of. This will result in a proper harmony between the body and the mind. They will work as one entity instead of two.

What we also fail to understand is the amount of junk we talk in front of our children. They do not need to hear all our conversations and neither do they need to know what is going on in our lives at all points of times. They need to have an independent thought process that is not interrupted by our thoughts and sentences. Kids tend to pick up on our views and make them their own and most times we take pride in that. This is just the opposite of what should be happening.

They have their own experiences to live; give them a chance to form their own views. In fact, as mentioned earlier, let them not 'form' any view but keep changing their perspective with all kinds of situations so that they know more about themselves and can grow in a much better fashion. So when you are in the company of your children, turn off that cell phone or go to the other room and talk your 'very important' talks or scream at that sales call. Because they listen to every word you are saying – consciously or unconsciously – and this will leave a negative (more often than not) mark on their subconscious.

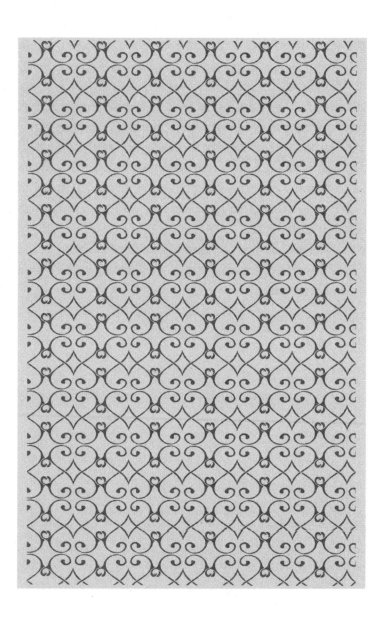

# 21

# A Message from the Angels About the Authors

$W$hy a book fails is part of a problem that has not been found by the authors.

An author never writes from his mind. Yes, he uses it, but he largely writes from his heart. Now, you would think in the case of this book, the writers are merely using their hands and their concentration and not their hearts or their minds. But in a way, it is not true.

Writing something that you don't even know will ever get published or will ever be read, is a very difficult proposition for these two loving young authors. They can't decide for themselves if it is a good thing that they are doing or whether all that they are doing is in vain. That is why they stop writing and stop believing from time to time. That is also why the book is taking longer to finish than we had imagined.

Everything they write, they need to feel as if they have contributed to it. It is their thoughts that match with ours and that is why they write what we tell them to write. But they don't know what is going to be written next. Neither do they know how the book is shaping up. So they get discouraged and stop writing. Dear friends, we have to tell you this for the sake of our writers – that they are writing without their minds and their thoughts interfering – and that is why they are able to write so beautifully. To do so is not an easy task and they need to know that the world at large is waiting to read the words that have been channelled through them.

They also write with their hearts because, when they sit to write a fresh new page, it is with the sole intention of writing purely and without using their own logic and judgement. So, we salute these two young friends of ours, who need a boost of confidence every now and then. After all, it is us who are making them write and so, they should trust us more than they trust themselves. We know what's good for them and we know how they will achieve what they want.

# Conclusion

$Y$ou have come to a stage when all of you understand what has been going wrong in your ways of living your life. You have started to understand what you need to do going forward and also know how to get there. If you have read carefully you would also know that there is much learning we could accomplish while we enjoy the earth plane.

So what's missing? The answer is – *Nothing*. This is it, our dear friends. Always remember that there is help at hand. Seek out and ask for help or rather command the universe to do what you need or desire. The true intents would unfold in front of your eyes.

Your conscience has so far played an altogether important

role to tell you what's right and what's wrong. It has given us judgement to choose wisely what's best for others and ourselves. Yet, we have now understood the limitations and grief our conscience can bring to our purpose in life. We are at the mercy of our conscience to reach our destiny. The power of this learning is not knowing the path but following it. I would urge all of you to reread the book or a couple of chapters after every few months or so to remind you what we are here for.